My Jewish World

An Introduction to Judaism

BEHRMAN HOUSE

My Jewish World

PEOPLE

PLACES

THINGS

ACTIONS

Robert Thum and Susan Dworski

Dedication

To the memory of Annette E. Thum,
who did so much to shape her family's Jewish values.

Editorial Board

Copyright © 1989 by Behrman House, Inc.
235 Watchung Avenue
West Orange, New Jersey 07052

ISBN: 0-87441-478-4

MANUFACTURED IN THE UNITED STATES OF AMERICA

Contents

Jewish People

CHAPTER 1

The Rabbi

Imagine your synagogue as one very large family. Think about the men and women who belong to your congregation and the girls and boys who go to school with you. They are like members of your family—like brothers and sisters and cousins and aunts. Just as families need parents to help and to care and to teach, so the synagogue needs a rabbi.

In some very important ways, the rabbi is like the congregation's father or mother.

The rabbi will recite a special blessing for you during the synagogue service celebrating your Bat or Bar Mitzvah.

Parents teach their children, and teaching children and grown-ups is one of the most important things the rabbi does. We must learn to be honest and kind. God wants us to tell the truth and to keep our promises. God wants us to be good to one another. These are some of the things the rabbi teaches us.

One of the ways the rabbi teaches is by presenting a lesson during services in the synagogue. This lesson is called a **sermon.** In the sermon, the rabbi may remind us to follow God's commandments, the **Mitzvot.**

What does the rabbi teach us about Mitzvot?

When we do a Mitzvah, we fulfill God's commandment. Sometimes a Mitzvah is a private commandment. It is just between you and God. When you love God with all your heart, you are performing a Mitzvah. Sometimes a commandment is between you and another person. When you give time or money to help someone in need, you are performing an important Mitzvah called **Tzedakah.**

Getting to Know Your Rabbi

Today you are going to be a reporter for the synagogue bulletin. It is your job to learn more about your rabbi and to write an article so that other members of your congregation can know the rabbi better too. You will be able to find out some answers from your parents or from people who work in your synagogue. You may have to ask your rabbi some questions too. Remember, a good reporter works hard to write an interesting story.

Rabbi _____

is the religious leader of _____,

located in _____,

Rabbi _____ was

graduated from _____

(University/College). After graduation, Rabbi received

(his/her) rabbinic training at _____

_____ in _____.

Rabbi _____

has been leader of the congregation for _____

years. Rabbi is _____ (married/single)

and has _____ children. Our rabbi is very interested in

(music, art, education, archaeology, history, etc.) _____

_____ and _____.

The thing our rabbi worries about most is

_____

_____. The thing our rabbi likes best about being a rabbi

is _____

The rabbi performs many kinds of Mitzvot. Sometimes they are Mitzvot for happy times, and sometimes the Mitzvot are for sad times. Think about the most important events in your life and in the life of your family. You will see that the rabbi has shared these happy and sad times with you.

Before the wedding ceremony begins, the rabbi watches the groom sign the marriage contract. It is called a **ketubah.** It contains the date and place of the wedding and the names of the bride and groom. The rabbi will read the ketubah aloud during the ceremony.

A family begins when a woman and a man, like your mother and father, decide to marry. Before a wedding takes place, the rabbi talks with the bride and groom about how to have a good Jewish home and a happy family life. The rabbi conducts the wedding ceremony. The cycle of life continues when a baby is born. The rabbi announces the birth at the synagogue service and names the new baby in a beautiful religious ceremony. When children enter religious school, in some synagogues the rabbi welcomes them at a service called a consecration. When boys and girls prepare to become a Bar or Bat Mitzvah, the rabbi shares the celebration. In synagogues where there is a confirmation ceremony for boys and girls when they are 15 or 16 years old, the rabbi is with them then too. And when these young people are ready to be married, they come to the rabbi and the cycle of life starts all over again.

The Rabbi Says

The rabbi shares the happy and the sad times in the life of a family. When will the rabbi say these things?

"PRAISED BE GOD WHO CAUSES THE GROOM TO REJOICE WITH HIS BRIDE."

"MAY HER PARENTS RAISE HER TO THE STUDY OF TORAH AND THE PERFORMANCE OF GOOD DEEDS."

"HIS MEMORY LIVES IN THE HEARTS OF HIS DEAR ONES."

"MAY GOD BLESS YOU AND KEEP YOU. MAY GOD SHOW YOU KINDNESS AND GIVE YOU PEACE."

AT A BAR MITZVAH

AT A FUNERAL

AT A BABY NAMING

AT A WEDDING

Families especially need their parents in times of trouble and sorrow. Sometimes the Mitzvot the rabbi performs are for these sad times. When someone is seriously ill, the rabbi visits along with family and friends. Visiting the sick is an important Mitzvah. It is called **bikkur ḥolim.** When we visit friends who are ill, we help them to get well again.

When there is a death in the family, there is a funeral service. The rabbi is with the family during this very sad time.

The rabbi performs an important Mitzvah by visting patients in the hospital. When people are very sick, the rabbi knows how to comfort them.

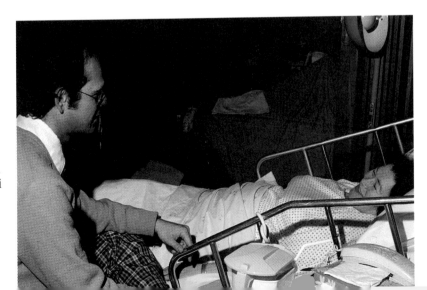

13

Teaching is one of the most important things the rabbi does. For Jews, learning continues even when we are grown-up. Here the rabbi teaches a class for adults like your own mother and father.

The rabbi helps the members of the congregation. When we have important decisions to make, such as which college to attend or which career to follow, the rabbi can help us make good choices. When we have problems, the rabbi knows how to help. If a couple is having trouble with their marriage, the rabbi will meet with them. When people can't agree, it is good to have someone who can listen

How does the rabbi teach important Jewish lessons?

The Torah commands us to do what is just and what is right. The rabbi shows us how to put Jewish teaching into action. Our rabbis care about all people everywhere. They work to feed the hungry and to shelter the homeless. They demonstrate to help free Jews who live in the Soviet Union and raise money to settle Jews in Israel. Our rabbis teach us important Jewish lessons not only with words, but by their actions.

You Be The Rabbi

Choose one of these lessons. Tell what you can do to put these Torah words into action.

carefully to both sides of an argument and make suggestions. Should the couple divorce, the rabbi helps both parents to stay close to the synagogue. The rabbi tries to be patient and wise. Your rabbi is a good person to talk to when you have a problem.

Not every rabbi works in a synagogue. Some rabbis teach courses and lead religious and social activities for students on college campuses.

15

A rabbi becomes wise by studying. It takes a long time and hard work to earn the title of rabbi and to have a congregation of your own. To become a rabbi you must study at a school called a **seminary.** Many rabbinical students also spend a year studying in Israel as part of their training.

When students finish their work, after as many as six years of study after college, they are **ordained.** This means that they are ready to share their learning by teaching others. From then on the student will be called "Rabbi." Rabbi is a Hebrew word. Can you guess what it means? Rabbi means "my teacher."

In the past, only men could become rabbis. Today, women also study in the Reform, Conservative and Reconstructionist rabbinic schools.

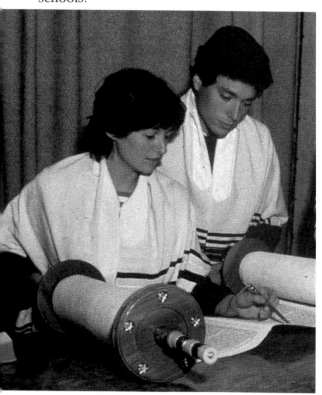

The Rabbi's Busy Day

The rabbi's day begins early in the morning and often doesn't end until late at night. Help the rabbi plan a day. Choose from the list of things to do, and fill in the rabbi's appointment book.

THINGS TO DO

Attend morning prayer service
Write a sermon
Teach adult Hebrew class
Meet with Reverend Johnson about shelter for the homeless
Visit residents at the home for the aged
Talk with Judy Cohen about her college application
Deliver eulogy at Dr. Levy's funeral
Attend Sisterhood luncheon
Study Talmud with Rabbi Friedman
Discuss Passover food collection with Men's Club Chairperson
Attend religious school assembly
Visit hospital patients
Jog three miles
Meet with bride and groom, Jessica Green and Robert Gelb
Call UJA office to schedule fund raising telethon
Read Jacob Gold's Bar Mitzvah speech
Visit nursery school class

APPOINTMENT CALENDAR

8:00

9:00

10:00

11:00

12:00

1:00

2:00

3:00

4:00

5:00

6:00

7:00

8:00

9:00

10:00

CHAPTER 2

The Cantor

Music is a very important part of our Jewish religion. We sing songs on every holiday and on Shabbat too. Music is a part of every prayer service in the synagogue. Your cantor is responsible for the music you hear and sing in your synagogue.

The cantor is sometimes called a **ḥazzan** or **ḥazzanit.** This Hebrew word means to oversee. Together, the rabbi and the cantor oversee, or lead us in community prayer.

Sometimes the cantor sings the prayers just as they have been chanted for many, many years. A special chant called **nusaḥ** is used. Sometimes the cantor may choose from several melodies.

Jewish music has a long, long history.

In the Bible we can read the words of the song the people of Israel sang after crossing the Red Sea. We still sing this song in the synagogue today. Songs were sung on the steps of the ancient Temple in Jerusalem, and musical instruments were played inside the Temple. There were trumpets and harps, strings and flutes, cymbals and drums. The most famous composer of prayer songs was King David. His songs are called psalms. David loved music, and he loved prayer.

Your cantor will help you prepare for your Bar or Bat Mitzvah. You will learn to read from the Torah and to chant your Haftarah portion that comes from the Prophets. Each of these readings has a different set of melodies.

Write Your Own Prayer

Think of something that makes you happy and write your own words to thank God. Can you sing the words?

I thank God for

I hope that

In a printed Bible, the **trop** is shown with small accent marks. The marks are like musical notes. They show a tune for each of the words so we will know how to sing them. Sometimes the marks appear above the letters. One looks like the English letter S on its side. Another has a diamond shape. Can you find them? Sometimes the marks appear underneath the letters. One looks like the English letter L, but it is backwards. Another looks like the letter U, but it is upside down. Do you see them? How many other accent marks can you find?

A very old kind of Jewish music is the chant we use to read the Torah and the Haftarah. We call this chant **trop.** The cantor chants trop as exactly as possible, a job which requires careful study of the Torah. When you prepare for your Bar or Bat Mitzvah, your cantor will help you learn to chant trop.

מֻנַּח זַרְקָא מֻנַּח סֶגּוֹל מֻנַּח ׀ מֻנַּח

רְבִיעִׂי מַהְפַּך פַּשְׁטָא זָקֵף־קָטֹן זָקֵף

גָּדֹול מֵרְכָא טִפְחָא מֻנַּח אֶתְנַחְתָּא

We love to sing our prayers, and some songs are very precious to us. The melody for Kol Nidre gives us a very serious feeling each year on the eve of Yom Kippur. The cantor asks God to set aside all the promises we will make to God but can not keep. The melody helps to make the words mean more. Each melody adds something different. A bright melody, like the tune of Sim Shalom, makes us all feel happy. The melody for Barechu helps us to feel that the time has come to pray together. Some prayers have many different melodies. How many tunes do you know for Adon Olam?

Name That Tune

Help the cantor choose the correct melody by filling in the missing letters of the title of each prayer.

ADON OLA____

BARECH____

SIM ____HALOM

KOL N____DRE

L'____HAH DODI

Use the five letters to complete this sentence:

THE CANTOR IS RESPONSIBLE FOR THE __ __ __ __ __
YOU HEAR AND SING IN THE SYNAGOGUE.

The melodies the cantor sings help you to concentrate on the words of the prayers. This concentration is called **kavanah** in Hebrew. Kavanah is what you do inside yourself to make your prayers come from your own heart. The cantor helps you to have kavanah by singing beautiful songs in much the same way that artists help you to understand more about life by painting colorful pictures that make you think.

Being a cantor is a very creative job.

Sometimes cantors compose new music to accompany the prayers. This is not an easy thing to do. It requires much more than just putting together enough notes to fit the words. The melody has to fit the meaning of the prayer too. When the song fits, the music and the words together make the meaning of the prayer clear. When the cantor brings new music to the old words of the prayerbook, the old words also seem new.

The cantor often teaches Jewish music in the religious school and to members of the youth group.

Cantors teach us new Hebrew songs. Singing together after dinner makes us all feel happy.

There are women cantors and men cantors. Their voices are very different. Imagine how you might feel listening to a male cantor sing the Shema in a deep baritone voice. Now try to imagine how you would feel hearing a female cantor sing the Shema in a high soprano voice.

Word Search

P	S	A	L	M	S	T	N
B	H	A	Z	Z	A	N	U
R	E	T	R	O	P	V	S
L	M	U	S	I	C	X	A
K	A	V	A	N	A	H	H
S	B	A	R	E	C	H	U

Look across and down to find eight words you know. Circle each one as you find it.

Use the words to complete the sentences. King David composed prayer songs called ___ ___ ___ ___ ___ ___.

The cantor is sometimes called a ___ ___ ___ ___ ___ ___.

___ ___ ___ ___ is the chant we use to read the Torah and the Haftarah.

___ ___ ___ ___ ___ is a very important part of our Jewish religion.

___ ___ ___ ___ ___ ___ ___ is what you do inside yourself to make your prayers come from your own heart.

The melody for ___ ___ ___ ___ ___ ___ ___ helps us to feel that the time has come to pray together.

The ___ ___ ___ ___ ___ is the most important Jewish prayer.

When the cantor sings the prayers just as they have been chanted for many years, a special chant called ___ ___ ___ ___ ___ is used.

There is much for a cantor to know and understand. Cantors attend a special school called a cantorial school. It is a place very much like the seminary where a rabbi studies. At cantorial school, students study Jewish music and prayer and learn all about the Jewish way of life.

The cantor must know all about Jewish music and have a fine singing voice to perform well.

Besides their work at the synagogue, cantors share their musical talents at many public occasions. When people marry they sing at weddings and when people die they sing at funeral services. They visit homes for the aged to play music and sing for the residents who are too ill to attend the synagogue. They often spend time at Jewish summer camps, teaching campers new songs and maybe even how to play the guitar or the harmonica.

The cantor's day is filled with many different tasks—very much like the rabbi's—but what a cantor most looks forward to is singing. By lifting their voices in song, cantors bring us—and themselves— closer to God.

Fill In The Blanks

Use these words to fill in the blank spaces in the sentences below.

David   Haftarah   Temple   funeral
Bar or Bat   blessings   singing   trop
hazzan   kavanah   compose   choir

1. Sometimes a cantor is called a _____, which means overseer.
2. Many cantors _____ their own music for the synagogue prayers.
3. King _____ wrote prayer songs called psalms.
4. Songs were sung on the steps of the ancient _____ in Jerusalem.
5. Your cantor will help you study and prepare for your _____ Mitzvah.
6. The cantor will teach you to chant the _____ portion that comes from the Prophets
7. The special chant used to read the Torah and the Haftarah is called _____
8. Sometimes the cantor acts as the _____ director.
9. The cantor sings seven _____ during the wedding ceremony.
10. The cantor sings a memorial prayer at _____ services.
11. _____ is what you do inside yourself to make your prayers come from your own heart.
12. What cantors look forward to most is _____

Your parents fulfill an important Mitzvah by sending you to a Jewish school.

CHAPTER 3

Your Principal and Teachers

Teaching young people is the most important part of Judaism. In the Bible, we are commanded to teach the Law of God to children: "And these words, which I command you this day, shall be upon your heart. You shall teach them diligently to your children."

The religious school is the part of your synagogue made especially for you. Your principal and your teachers have held meetings with your parents and other parents in the congregation. Together with your rabbi and your cantor they have organized the school in which you now study. They work hard to make it a good school and an interesting one.

25

Some Words About Books

Books are very important to our people. Here are some Jewish quotations about books. Pick one quotation and in your own words, write what it means to you.

Your principal meets with the school committee to decide what will be taught in your school. All the different subjects you will study are called the school curriculum. You will study the Bible and Jewish history. You will study Jewish customs and holidays and the Hebrew language. There is so much to learn! All this knowledge is contained in books. Your principal chooses the books you read in school, like this one. There are Purim and Ḥanukkah parties and other happy times. Your principal wants to make learning about Judaism interesting and fun—because Judaism is interesting and fun!

66One should not leap through a book
from its end to its beginning." (TALMUD, YOMA)

66Books are pouches of wisdom embroidered
with pearly words." (MOSHE BEN EZRA)

66Keep your books well. Keep them from the rain above,
from mice and any other damage, because
they are your precious treasure." (YEHUDA IBN TIBBON)

66A book is the most pleasant of friends." (AVRAHAM BEN EZRA)

66Books are meant not be to shelved, but
to be studied." (SEFER HAHASIDIM)

66A good book is like a beautiful garden
that you can carry in your hand." (HANANYA REICHMAN)

_____

_____

_____

_____

_____

Your principal or educational director chooses the books you study. Just as a carpenter needs proper tools, so a student needs good books!

Educational directors and teachers often visit other schools and attend meetings around the country to talk with other principals and teachers. They are always looking for new textbooks. Teachers are always learning new ways to teach young people like you.

The teachers in your school are hired by your principal. Some of the teachers are young, and maybe you know some who are studying to become rabbis or cantors. Some of the teachers are older and have taught for many years. They have dedicated their lives to Jewish learning.

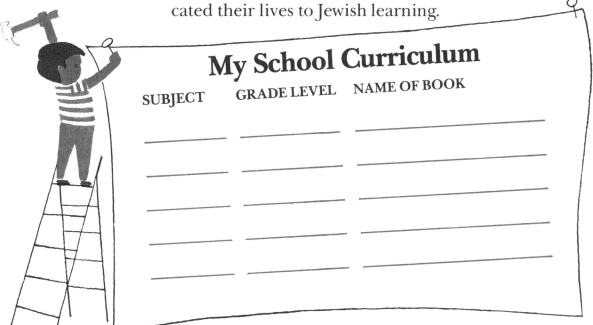

My School Curriculum

SUBJECT	GRADE LEVEL	NAME OF BOOK

For Jews learning doesn't stop when we are grown-up. Learning is a life-long activity. Jewish people learn as much as we can. The educational director of your religious school and your teachers continue their own studies and teach adult classes too. After dark, when you are at home tucked into bed, your principal and your teacher are busy teaching Hebrew to grownups—maybe your own mother and father.

The sweetness of learning.

Long ago there was a Jewish custom that when children began school, their first lesson was covered with honey. When they licked it, they could taste the "sweetness" of Jewish study. Today, your teacher looks for new ways to encourage you to learn.

Your teachers make learning about Judaism interesting and fun.

What Kind of Student Are You?

Our rabbis have said that there are four kinds of students:

1 The first is the one who is quick to understand and quick to forget.

2 The next student is slow to understand and slow to forget.

3 The third student is quick to understand and slow to forget.

4 The last kind of student is slow to understand and quick to forget.

Which student is like a funnel?

Which student is like a sponge?

Which student is best?

_____

_____

_____

_____

When you think of your teachers, the ones you probably think of first are the ones who teach in the classroom—but there are others. Your synagogue youth group leader is your teacher too. Your parents teach you Jewish things at home, and your counselors teach you Jewish things at summer camp. Not all Jewish learning takes place in the classroom.

My Teachers

Think about the people who have taught you in school. Then think about the many others who help you learn important things. Which teachers have been the most important to you?

Being an American Jew today is an important responsibility. All of your teachers, your rabbi, your cantor and your parents want to help you understand "why." They make your Jewish school and your synagogue an exciting place in which to learn.

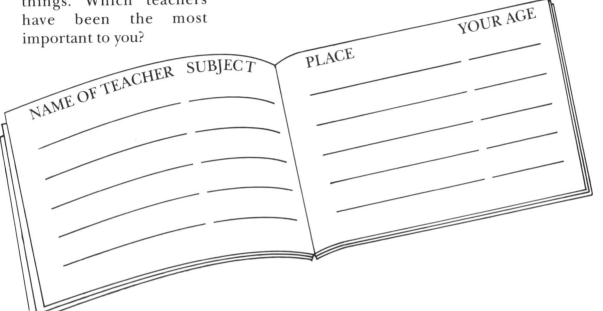

NAME OF TEACHER   SUBJECT   PLACE   YOUR AGE

Our rabbis have said that there are four kinds of students. What kind of student are you?

Other people work in the synagogue.

It takes many people to make a synagogue run smoothly. The building needs to be kept clean and tidy. That's the job of the custodian. There are bills to be paid. That's the bookkeeper's job. The secretary answers the phone and takes care of the mail. The synagogue is a busy place. There are many activities to schedule and celebrations to plan. In many synagogues, it is the executive director who keeps things running smoothly.

Some people work in the synagogue as volunteers. They give their time without being paid. Volunteers work in the library, the gift shop and sometimes in the school too. Their contribution is important. It is very expensive to maintain a building, an office and a school. Everyone can volunteer to help—even you!

You are an important part of the synagogue. You celebrate the holidays with your parents by attending services. You go to religious school and later you will study for your Bar or Bat Mitzvah. Your teachers will help you and your classmates prepare to take part in the Jewish community as you grow up. It will be up to you to decide what is right and what is wrong. Your understanding of Judaism will help you to decide. Students like you and your classmates will keep Judaism alive in the future.

Help Deliver The Goods

In a big synagogue there are many offices and rooms. Help deliver the supplies to the right place by drawing a line from each thing to the room where it is needed.

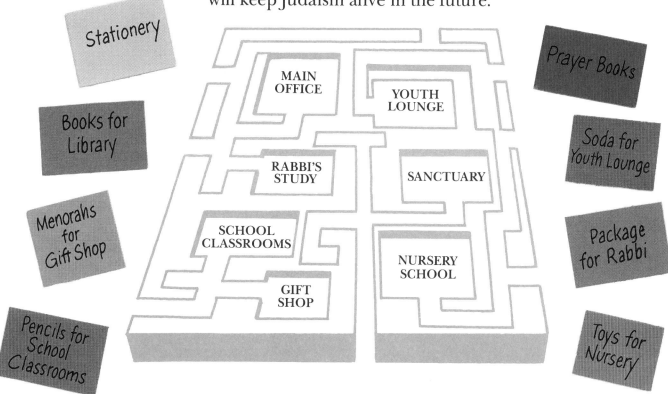

Stationery

Prayer Books

Books for Library

Soda for Youth Lounge

Menorahs for Gift Shop

Package for Rabbi

Pencils for School Classrooms

Toys for Nursery

MAIN OFFICE

YOUTH LOUNGE

RABBI'S STUDY

SANCTUARY

SCHOOL CLASSROOMS

NURSERY SCHOOL

GIFT SHOP

We are always welcome in the land of Israel. Even when we do not live there, Israel is the second home for Jews everywhere. Some young people celebrate their Bat or Bar Mitzvah in Jerusalem.

CHAPTER **4** # Am Yisrael

When you look up at the clear night sky, you can see millions of twinkling stars. Some of the stars stand out brightly in small, separate groups. Others are crowded so close together they look like thick, white clouds.

These faraway stars are like the Jewish people. God made a promise to our ancestor Abraham long, long ago. God promised that our people would be like "the stars of the heavens." And today, 13 million Jews live in almost every country in the world. In large cities and in small communities, rabbis teach, cantors lead prayer services, and young people like you study in Jewish schools. We are all joined together as one people—**Am Yisrael.**

Where Do They Live?

Today, Jews live in almost every country in the world. In several countries, there are very large numbers of Jewish people. These are shown by stars on the map. Color in the stars to see where most Jews live.

More than 1,000,000   100,000 to 1,000,000   50,000 to 100,000

Most Jews in the world live in the United States, Israel and Russia. Other Jews live in England, South America, Africa and even Australia. When Jews live in free countries, we can worship God in our synagogues and study Torah and the Hebrew language in our own schools. In countries like the United States, Canada and England, we are treated as equals in our everyday lives.

33

In some other places, Jews are not as lucky. In the Soviet Union, Russian Jews have not been allowed to print Jewish books or newspapers. It has been against the law to train new rabbis, and it was even forbidden to bake matzah for Passover! Things may be getting better in the Soviet Union. We pray that Russian Jews will soon be able to practice their religion freely.

Young students like you march for the United Jewish Appeal. The money they raise will help Jews all over the world.

Life is very hard for Jews in Russia.

Many Russian Jews wish to move to Israel or to the United States. They want to begin a new life for themselves and for their children. But it is not easy to get permission to leave Russia. The government must give you an "exit visa," a piece of paper that says you are free to leave. Jews must apply to the government again and again over many years. In the meantime, they often lose their jobs. They are refused so often that they have been given a special name. They are called "refuseniks."

34

Getting Out

Imagine that you are a Russian Jew. You want to emigrate to Israel to begin a new life. You must fill out many forms to get permission to leave. Complete the form.

EMIGRATION VISA REQUEST

Name _____

Address _____

City _____

Place of birth _____

Age _____

Nationality _____

Occupation _____

Present job _____

_____

Why do you want to leave the Soviet Union? _____

_____

Russia is not the only place where Jewish people are struggling to keep our Jewish ways. For a very long time, a group of Jews lived in a small country in Arabia called Yemen. These Jews, called Yemenites, lived almost the same way as the Hebrews lived in the days of the Bible.

The Jews of Yemen had long wished to live in the land of Israel. They held the belief that God would bring them home to Israel "on the wings of eagles." In 1950 their dream came true. The newly formed State of Israel sent airplanes to rescue the Jews of Yemen. Most of them had never even seen an airplane before! Can you imagine how the Yemenite Jews felt as they boarded big "silver birds" to fly to their new home in Israel?

35

Most Yemenite Jews are now settled in Israel.

Today, young Yemenite Jews look and dress like other modern Israelis. But during certain holidays and celebrations, they dress in traditional Yemenite clothing. The women wear beautiful embroidered dresses and caps, and lots of silver and gold jewelry. The men wear the long robes of Arabia.

This bride and groom are dressed for their traditional Yemenite wedding ceremony.

These two children were brought to Israel by "Operation Moses." They are now happily settled in their new home.

Another airlift rescue took place more recently. This rescue mission had a special code name. It was called "Operation Moses." In 1985 Israeli jets flew across northern Africa to a country called Sudan. Sudan is next to Ethiopia, where thousands of Jews were starving to death during a terrible famine. The Ethiopian government did not want to let the Jews leave. They had to escape secretly, trekking hundreds of miles across desert and mountains to Sudan. In a series of daring airlifts, Israeli pilots flew many of these Ethiopian Jews to Israel. Sadly, just as many could not make the trip and are still suffering in Ethiopia. Can you figure out why this rescue mission was called "Operation Moses"?

Find The Escape Route

In order to escape, the Ethiopian Jews had to walk for long, dangerous distances to reach Sudan where Israeli pilots waited to take them to Israel. Help them find their way.

This man lives in Tunisia, a country in North Africa. On the holiday of Sukkot, he joins Jewish people all over the world, shaking the lulav to show that God is everywhere.

ISRAEL

SUDAN

ETHIOPIA

Our Jewish Homeland

The land of Israel is very old. Jewish people have lived there for thousands of years. But the State of Israel is very young. It was founded in the year 1948. Each spring we celebrate Israel's birthday on a holiday called Yom Ha-atzmaut. The State of Israel has its own national anthem. The song is called "Hatikvah," the Hebrew word for "the hope." We hoped that Israel would be a country where any Jewish person could live. We are happy that this dream is coming true. How old will Israel be on its birthday this year?

Design A Banner

Design a banner to make and proudly carry in the Yom Ha-atzmaut parade.

We celebrate Israel Independence Day with great joy. In Israel, and in Jewish communities around the world, there are happy parades. We feel proud on this day—proud of the State of Israel and proud to be Jewish.

Jews in different countries around the world often follow their own local customs. These customs most often have to do with food and clothing, or ways of celebrating Jewish holidays. In Israel Purim is celebrated as a national holiday. There are parades with floats and marching bands. In parts of Europe Purim is celebrated with masquerade parties in which women may dress up as men, and men as women.

Although Jewish customs may differ, God's commandments—the Mitzvot—do not change easily. Shabbat is always Shabbat, although a Russian family may light only one candle instead of two. Yom Kippur is always Yom Kippur, even though synagogue services may be different for Reform, Conservative and Orthodox congregations. Different customs help people feel more at home in their particular community, but the Mitzvot unite all Jewish people around the world.

Tonight, look up into the dark sky. You will see all sorts of stars shining there. Ask yourself, are these "stars" all the same? Not really. There are planets and meteors. There are shimmering "stars" that are really nothing more than swirls of radiant gas. But they all shine with the same light.

The world is like the night sky and the Jewish people are like the stars in it. We may not look or dress the same way. We may live in different lands and follow different customs. But we all shine with the same light—our study of Torah, our concern for Israel and for all people everywhere, and our love of God.

Multiple Choice

Circle the word that best completes the sentence.

1. There are _____ million Jews in the world today. 100 13 49

2. Jews are all joined together as one people called _____ Yisrael. Am Rabbi Shema

3. Jewish people are not allowed to practice our religion in _____.

America North Africa Russia

4. We hold large _____ here to help the Jews in Russia. boxes rallies picnics

5. Jews who ask for permission to leave Russia may become _____.

refuseniks Ethiopians Yemenites

6. The Jews of Yemen believed that they would be brought to Israel on the "wings of _____." song airplanes eagles

7. The rescue mission that brought Ethiopian Jews to Israel was called "Operation _____." Moses Sudan Eagle

8. The national anthem of the State of Israel is called _____.

Barechu trop Hatikvah

9. The State of Israel's birthday is celebrated on a holiday called _____.

Yom Kippur Shabbat Yom Ha-atzmaut

10. God's commandments, the _____, unite all Jewish people around the world.

Mitzvot nusah custom

UNIT II

Jewish Places

CHAPTER 5

The Synagogue

There are all kinds of synagogues. Some are large buildings with high ceilings and wonderful decorations. Others are small buildings, and very plain inside. But no matter how large or small, all synagogues are places where Jews come together to meet, to study and to pray.

Sometimes a synagogue is called a House of Meeting—**Bet Knesset.** Sometimes a synagogue is called a House of Study—**Bet Midrash.** And sometimes a synagogue is called a House of Prayer—**Bet Tefillah.**

Some synagogues have windows made from many pieces of stained glass. The rainbow colors of sunlight coming through these windows help to make praying together in the synagogue a warm and beautiful experience.

43

The synagogue at Capernaum was used during Roman times, 2,000 year ago!

In ancient times, Jews worshipped in a great stone Temple in Jerusalem. When our Temple was destroyed almost 2,000 years ago, we lost our own land, and we spread out and settled among the different peoples in many lands. Our people continued to meet, to study Torah and to read and discuss God's laws. We carried our Torah with us everywhere we went and we built synagogues for study and for worship everywhere we lived.

What were ancient synagogues like?

One of the most famous ancient synagogues is in Israel at a place called Capernaum. This was a large synagogue, and it was decorated with beautiful designs made with thousands and thousands of little pieces of colored stone. These stone decorations are called mosaics. The mosaic floor of the Capernaum synagogue is still there, and pieces of walls and columns are still standing. Other ancient synagogues have been found in Egypt, in Syria and in Italy. In one of them, a stone **bimah** was discovered. A bimah is the platform from which the Torah is read to the congregation—even today.

Create a Mosaic

A mosaic is made by putting together many small pieces of colored stone, glass, or tile. Color in the spaces to create your own mosaic.

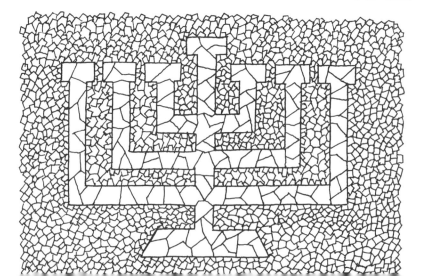

Today in the synagogue we study Torah and the words of the Prophets. We study Hebrew and history. We listen to the rabbi's sermons, and we study together in the religious school. You will prepare for your Bar or Bat Mitzvah in your synagogue. Adults study there too. If you have noticed the word "study" being used many times to describe the synagogue, you have been reading carefully. Remember that a synagogue is called Bet Midrash or House of Study.

In your synagogue there may be a **menorah** with seven branches. Some people think that the branches stand for the seven days of Creation. The middle branch represents the Sabbath day—Shabbat. How is this menorah different from the one we light on Ḥanukkah?

At a Bet Midrash people of all ages come to learn and to teach. Jews believe that not only children like you, but grown-ups too must continue to study. Have you ever seen a gray-haired grandfather studying in the synagogue library while an eight year-old granddaughter struggles to learn the first letters of the alef bet in a nearby classroom? Just because you're older, doesn't mean there's nothing left to learn. In fact, the more you understand about Judaism, the more you want to learn!

45

The Synagogue Gift Shop

The synagogue gift shop makes many Jewish items available to members of the congregation and to the community. Imagine that you are the buyer for the synagogue gift shop. It is your job to choose the items to be offered for sale. Of course, as in any business, you have a budget. You have $200 to spend. Study the items carefully and then figure out what you will buy to stock the gift shop. You can choose more than one of an item if you think it will sell well. Use scratch paper or a calculator to compute the total amount of your purchases.

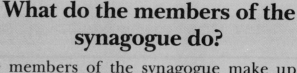

What do the members of the synagogue do?

The members of the synagogue make up a congregation. The women in the congregation may also belong to the Sisterhood or Women's League. The Sisterhood often helps the religious school, raises money for the youth group and runs the gift shop. The men in the congregation may belong to the Brotherhood or Men's Club. They help with prayer services and plan interesting programs. Sometimes they help sponsor television broadcasts so many more people can study and learn. Children attend religious school and teenagers belong to the youth group. Everyone in the congregation helps one another. They also help other people in the community.

$40

$45

$15

$15

$10

$20

One of the other names for a synagogue is Bet Tefillah or House of Prayer. No matter how big or how small the building, every synagogue has a main room where members gather together to pray. It is called the **sanctuary.** At the front of the sanctuary is the Holy Ark or **Aron Hakodesh.** Inside the Ark we keep the scrolls of the Torah. When the Torah is read it is placed on a desk on the bimah, the platform in front of the Ark. If you look closely the next time you are in your synagogue sanctuary, no matter what time of day or night it is, you will see a

The **Ner Tamid** hangs above the Holy Ark. It never goes out. This reminds us that God always watches over us.

lamp flickering above the Ark. This is the **Ner Tamid** or the Eternal Light. It burns all day and all night.

Many activities take place in the synagogue. Weddings are celebrated. Bar and Bat Mitzvahs are observed. Prayer services may be held each morning and the congregation comes together to pray on Friday evening and on Shabbat morning. On holidays like Simḥat Torah and Yom Kippur, the sanctuary is filled to overflowing with people who have come to worship.

The synagogue is also a Bet Knesset, or House of Meeting. The members of the congregation meet in the synagogue to discuss important ideas. These discussions are often lively and loud. Sometimes the members even argue. Arguing about ideas is one of the ways people learn and grow. Can you think of an argument that helped you learn something important?

Synagogue Dictionary

Match the word to its meaning. Write each word next to the correct definition.

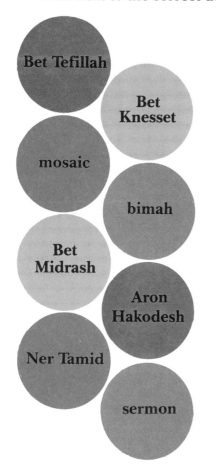

House of Meeting _____

House of Study _____

Talk the rabbi gives at services _____

House of Prayer _____

Holy Ark _____

designs made with pieces of colored stone ____

platform _____

Eternal Light _____

Your family and friends may lift you high on a chair and carry you as they dance around the social hall during your Bar or Bat Mitzvah party.

Jewish people love getting together to have a good time. We meet in the synagogue to have fun. If your synagogue has a social hall, there are probably dances for teenagers and holiday celebrations for families. Plays are performed on the stage and movies are shown. You can have your Bar or Bat Mitzvah party in the social hall.

At the synagogue, we meet, we study, we pray—and we celebrate important events in our lives, just as Jews have done for 2,000 years.

True or False

Put a T next to a true statement.
Put an F next to an untrue statement.

1. ___ A synagogue can be called a Bet Knesset, Bet Midrash, and Bet Tefillah.

2. ___ The word Bet Knesset means "big temple."

3. ___ All synagogues are big buildings.

4. ___ The word Bet Tefillah means "House of Prayer."

5. ___ Only children may study in a Bet Midrash.

6. ___ At night, we turn off the Ner Tamid.

7. ___ The cantor is in charge of the music in the synagogue.

8. ___ Only men are allowed to work in a synagogue.

9. ___ The Torah is kept in the Aron HaKodesh.

10. ___ Secretaries work in the synagogue's sanctuary.

11. ___ The bimah is a platform from which the Torah is read.

12. ___ The Sisterhood helps to raise money for the synagogue.

6

The Community Center

Can you think of a place where you can swim, learn how to do Israeli folk dances, and play basketball after school?

If you thought of the Jewish community center, you were right! In almost every city where many Jewish people live, you will find a Jewish community center. Sometimes it is called the YM-YWHA (which is an abbreviation for a long name: "**Y**oung **M**en's and **Y**oung **W**omen's **H**ebrew **A**ssociation").

If your father wants to learn some new Passover recipes, he can come to the Jewish community center for cooking classes.

If your sister wants to learn how to make Yemenite jewelry, she can learn in a crafts class at the community center.

If your chubby uncle and aunt want to lose weight, they can take an exercise class at the community center. (Maybe it will help!)

All kinds of things happen at the Jewish community center for people of all ages.

Your little brother can safely play at the Y's nursery school while your parents are working.

Jews who have just moved here from other countries can make new friends at the community center. They will feel at home speaking their native language while they learn English and our American ways.

Your great-grandparents can sit in the sun on the patio playing cards with their senior citizen friends. You may hear them speaking Yiddish. Sometimes they do it when they want to keep a secret from you, but mostly they do it because they love their native language.

How Do I Get There?

Find your way to the gym, the nursery school, the swimming pool, the auditorium and the crafts classroom.

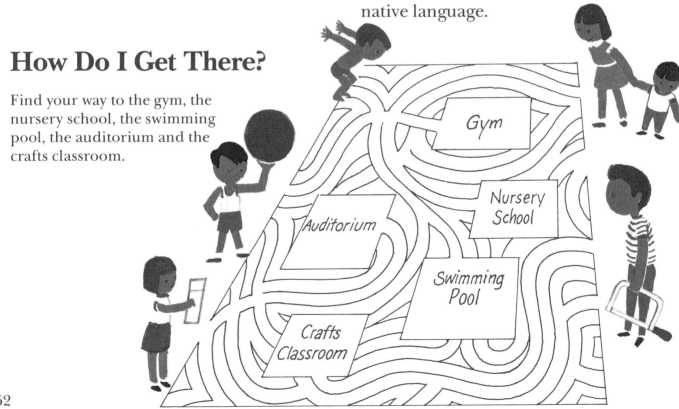

Gym

Nursery School

Auditorium

Swimming Pool

Crafts Classroom

The Y is a place for sports.

In some towns the Jewish community center has the very best facilities for sports like basketball and swimming. Maybe there is a jogging track too, or even a grassy field for playing soccer or football. Some people belong to the Y because they want to use these sport facilities. Everyone loves games and competing for fun.

People come to the community center because of the many different programs that take place there. Programs is another word for "things to do." The programs at the center are organized by the staff. The staff is all the people who work there. That includes your swimming instructor, your basketball coach, the dance teacher, and the executive director of the center.

Performing in a show at your Jewish community center is a good way to explore your musical talents.

Celebrations at the center include a Purim carnival with games to play, prizes to win and a contest for the best costume.

What's Happening?

You are member of the community center. Decide which activities you want to do. Check the bulletin board list and fill out your schedule.

ARTS AND CRAFTS
Grades 1–4
Learn to draw your favorite cartoon characters. Paint with sand. Make candles and other gifts for Mom and Dad.
Tuesday 4–6

COMPUTER COURSE
Grades 3–5
Learn to write Basic computer programs.
Monday 4–6

PLAY ACTING
Grades 3–6
Learn how to make scenery and costumes, do lighting and apply makeup. Perform in a play.
Wednesday 6–8

LET'S TALK HEBREW
Grades 3–7
Learn to speak Hebrew like an Israeli.
Sunday 1–2

SWIMMING
Grades 2–8
Improve your skills and prepare for swim team tryouts.
Sunday 1–3

DANCING
Grades 1–4
Bring your tap or ballet shoes and prepare for dance recital.
Thursday 4–6

CHINESE COOKING
Grades 3–4
Learn to cook in a wok, with easy kosher oriental recipes.
Wednesday 4–6

SOCCER
Grades 3–6
Develop control, running and endurance. Uniforms provided.
Sunday 1–3

BASKETBALL
Grades 3–5
Develop shooting skills and learn team work. Compete against other teams in Jewish community center league.
Sunday 2–4

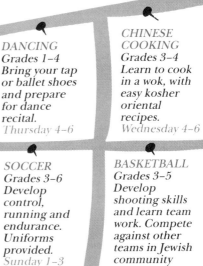

MY ACTIVITY SCHEDULE

ACTIVITY	DAY	TIME

At some centers you can meet a special person called a **shaliah.** The shaliah is a kind of "visiting expert" who is sent from Israel to learn more about America and to teach us more about Israel. If you have a shaliah at your Y, you will have a chance to get the answers to all your questions about Israel.

At the community center, Jewish people get together and dance and swim and cook and exercise and read and play games and perform plays and make art.

Sometimes we just talk.

At the center we can talk about the world and talk about ourselves. We talk about our love for Israel. We discuss current events. We wonder how many trees will be planted in Israel next year with the money raised at our center. We talk about the problems facing Russian Jews. We talk about new Jewish books. We talk about weddings and Bar and Bat Mitzvahs. We talk about our parents and our children and our grandchildren.

The Jewish community center is a friendly place where people can share their lives with each other. It is a place where we can relax and enjoy being together with other Jewish people who share our interests.

Young children learn to swim in the pool. The Y is a
place to develop new skills.

Some famous entertainers, musicians and actors got
their start by performing at their local Jewish community centers. So why don't you try out for a play,
or join a sports team, or learn folk dancing? You
don't have to worry when you drop the ball or step
on your dancing partner's toes! At the Jewish community center there is always someone nearby to
encourage you to try again.

You Be The Director

Pretend that you are the director of a Jewish community center. You are in charge of planning the programs for the coming year. Be sure to include activities and programs for members of every age group. When you have finished your list, compare it to your classmates' lists.

CHAPTER 7

The Home for the Aged

When people become very old, like great-grandparents, they are sometimes unable to take care of themselves. They become ill, or they fall down and break a hip, or maybe they just can't remember how to put their pajamas on.

A family may then get together and decide that it would be better for great-grandmother to live in a place where she will receive good care—in a home for the aged.

It is a difficult decision to make. We think about it for a long time. We worry about whether great-grandmother will be lonely. We wonder if there are good doctors and nurses to take care of the residents in the home. We visit to make sure that the rooms are clean and tidy, that there is plenty of fresh air, that there are nice people to talk to and that there are interesting things to do.

These residents are very proud of the decorations they are making for the home's sukkah.

We worry about how much it will cost to keep great-grandmother in the home, too. Usually, several members of the family contribute money each month to help pay for her new home. The local Jewish community and the federal government help too.

Hanging decorations in the sukkah is hard work for old people, but it's still lots of fun. You can help too.

59

Great-Grandmother's Room

When old people move to a home for the aged, it is very important that they be surrounded by familiar things that they love. The drawing of the room below is not very comfortable, is it? Use pencils and coloring pens to make it a happier place. Remember, little things like family photographs, slippers, a bedspread and a reading lamp are important. Don't forget a window to look out of!

On Friday evening, Shabbat services are a special time at a Jewish home for the aged.

There are many kinds of homes for the aged, but elderly Jews often choose to go to a Jewish one. If your great-grandmother keeps kosher, and only eats foods prepared according to the special Jewish dietary laws, she will certainly want to live in a Jewish home. Even if she does not observe all of the rules of **kashrut,** she will enjoy the Shabbat celebration on Friday evening and the holiday celebrations all through the year.

A rabbi or cantor leads prayer services.

The rabbi and cantor from the local synagogue will visit the home to lead prayer services on Jewish holidays and festivals. After services, they may stay for coffee and chat with great-grandmother and her friends, telling them what's going on in the synagogue and chatting with them about old friends. These visits will help great-grandmother still feel a part of the Jewish community.

Watering the pots in the home's greenhouse helps the plants to grow and bloom. When people become old, they are not always strong and active, but they still love life.

At a Jewish home for the aged, there are many interesting programs for the residents. Great-grandmother can knit and embroider, and maybe even learn to paint with watercolors. Holidays are happy times. There are apples to dip in honey for a sweet new year, a sukkah to decorate and Ḥanukkah candles to light.

What Can You Give?

Which gift would you bring for each of the people below?

You and your family can visit the home anytime you wish, on holidays, after school or on weekends. Even if you don't have a grandfather or a great-grandmother in the home for the aged, you can visit as a volunteer.

What can you do to help?

Sometimes elderly people's eyes are weak. You can read aloud the news from the daily paper. Or you can help with simple chores, like polishing shoes. Or maybe you can just sit and chat about your own activities—about school or your hobbies or your friends. Remember, old people still love life, even if they can't climb a tree or dance the hora.

A small bunch of fresh flowers can brighten an old person's day.

Fill In The Blanks

There are many things you can do as a volunteer at a home for the aged. Fill in the blank spaces below to help you remember.

Old people's eyes often become weak. It is sometimes difficult for them to see. Reading aloud is a nice thing to do when you visit a home for the aged.

When you visit elderly people at a home for the aged, you are fulfilling a Mitzvah, an act of kindness that is one of God's commandments. By your kindness, you are giving a gift of yourself that makes their lives happier and less lonely.

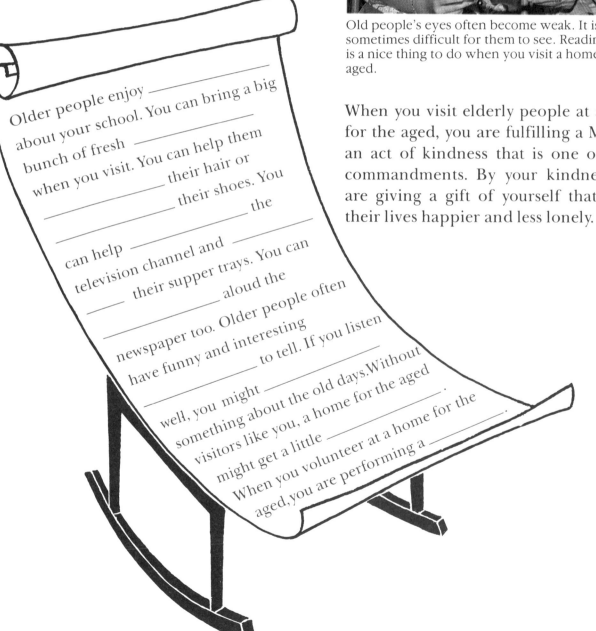

Older people enjoy _____ about your school. You can bring a big bunch of fresh _____ when you visit. You can help them _____ their hair or _____ their shoes. You can help _____ the television channel and _____ their supper trays. You can _____ aloud the newspaper too. Older people often have funny and interesting _____ to tell. If you listen well, you might _____ something about the old days. Without visitors like you, a home for the aged might get a little _____. When you volunteer at a home for the aged, you are performing a _____.

8

Summer Camp

Sam likes to play soccer. Leah likes to paint tee shirts. Mark likes to sing folk songs. Sharon likes to go swimming every day. Where can they do all these things together? At summer camp!

If your camp is by a lake or near a river, you can fish and learn to sail. If it is near the ocean, you can get up early in the morning and poke in the tidepools looking for starfish. If it is in the woods, you can hike and learn about nature.

Jewish camp is a great place to spend the summer.

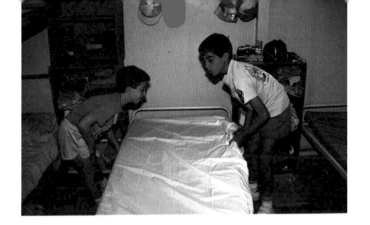

Sharing the work with your friends at camp is more fun than doing chores at home.

At camp everyone has a job to do. Sometimes these jobs are easy, like setting the tables before dinner or feeding the horses. But there are other jobs, like washing dishes and cleaning the bunks, that are harder to enjoy.

Some kids think that camp is like living on a **kibbutz.** A kibbutz is a Jewish farm community in Israel. Everyone shares the work equally on a kibbutz. Girls work in the fields sometimes, while boys do the laundry. Everybody pitches in and helps, just like in summer camp.

The people at camp are like a big family.

The camp director, the counselors and the other campers help kids overcome their fears and their homesickness. Helping others like this is called **hesed** in Hebrew. It means looking out for another person and paying special attention to friends who need help. Jewish camps often have special hesed projects. Perhaps in your camp you will write letters to Russia or make Shabbat candlesticks for Jewish patients in the local hospital.

Counselors help campers and older campers help younger kids. When you are kind and helpful and caring, remember the Hebrew word **ḥesed.**

Design A Camp Logo

Every camp has a special logo, or insignia. This logo is designed to illustrate the camp's name. For example, the insignia for *Camp Lone Pine* might have one pine tree and the moon in the sky. Here is a list of names of Jewish summer camps. Choose one that you like, or think of a name of your own, and design a logo in the circle. Then color it in. As you work, imagine how your logo would look on a tee shirt, or a duffel bag, or even on a sailboat. Would people be able to guess the camp's name if they saw your logo?

Camp names: SHALOM

HATIKVAH

RAINBOW

EAGLE COVE

WILDWOOD

SUNRISE LAKE

At summer camp you learn new crafts. You can learn how to weave a belt or make a menorah out of clay. You can learn to stencil a star of David on your tee shirt. You can make a Tzedakah box out of tree bark to collect money for the poor. And you can catch caterpillars and watch them spin their cocoons and turn into butterflies.

For day campers, the fun begins the moment they get on the camp bus. It's hard to leave at the end of a day filled with sports, swimming, crafts and Jewish activities.

When you begin to learn archery, you will probably miss the target more often than you will hit it. You may feel disappointed. You may get angry or want to quit. Instead, you make a secret promise to shoot straighter next time. Practice and practice. You will improve a little every day. By the time your parents arrive on visiting day, you'll be able to shoot all six arrows into the bull's-eye!

There are all kinds of special Jewish camps. You can learn to speak Hebrew, specialize in art or drama, learn all about computers or even lose weight.

Often, guests visit summer camp. Folk singers and dancers perform interesting programs about Israel.

One of the most exciting parts of Jewish camp is the sports competition. Sometimes it is called the Maccabiah. This is the name given to sport competitions in Israel. It comes from the brave Maccabees of our Ḥanukkah holiday. The competition may last for a day or even for a whole week. The Maccabiah games include sporting events and art and song contests too. It's a chance for kids of all ages to work and play together.

Song Contest

In the song contest, campers make up new words to sing along with old tunes. Can you write a song for the contest?

Here are some ideas to get you started.

These words fit the notes of *Oh My Darlin' Clementine*:

"T'was an owl, on the prowl,
Who had rabbits on his mind.
He had the habit
Of hunting rabbits,
All the rabbits, he could find."

Here's a sample that fits the notes of *She'll Be Coming 'Round the Mountain*:

"We will watch the dreidel turning as it spins.
We will watch the dreidel turning as it spins.
We will watch the dreidel spinning,
And we do hope we are winning! We will watch the dreidel turning as it spins."

And here's another that fits the notes of *You Are My Sunshine*:

"We light the candles
The Sabbath candles
We light them every Friday night
We light the candles
The Sabbath candles
It is such a lovely sight."

Praying is different at Jewish summer camp.

There is something wonderful about welcoming Shabbat outside under the evergreen trees. Everyone has a chance to take part. As you say the prayers, study the night sky. You can see many more stars than at home. Looking at the stars in the heavens has always made people feel closer to God. The stars remind us of God's promise to Abraham. Do you remember what that promise was?

One of the best things about summer camp is meeting kids from different places and finding out how other Jewish families live.

The last campfire of the summer is a sad time. Everyone sways arm-in-arm and hugs. The kids who were homesick have learned that they can live away from home. The scaredy-cats don't think that chipmunks are bears any more . . . and you've become a fine archer!

The next morning, as the campers board the buses to go home, everybody yells, "See you next year!"

The friendships you make during the summer can last all year long. Perhaps your parents still have friends they met at summer camp long ago.

CAMPFIRE STORY

Stories told around a crackling campfire after dark are
one of the things everybody remembers about summer
camp. Your mother and father may still remember some of
the stories they heard when they were at camp.

Fill in the blank spaces to create your own campfire story.
Make it as silly or as serious as you wish.

There once live an old _____ . It lived in a _____ and

ate _____ every night for dinner. One day, along came a teeny

little _____ dragging a big sack. "Would you like to buy some

delicious _____ for supper?" he asked.

   "Maybe," replied the old _____ .

   Then the teeny little _____ opened his sack and out

jumped a hundred million _____ . They _____ and

then disappeared into the _____ . The teeny little

_____ threw up his hands and _____ until he fell

asleep.

   While he slept, the old _____ took the empty sack and went

off into the _____ . He worked all night until the sack was full of

_____ . When the teeny little _____ awoke, he found

the filled sack. Lying next to it was the old _____ , fast asleep.

   The teeny little _____ was very grateful, but he did not want

to wake his new friend. Instead, he pinned a note to his shirt. The note

read: Thank you for your _____ , sir. It was an act of true

_____ .

UNIT **III**

Jewish Things

CHAPTER **9** **The Bible**

The Jewish people are sometimes known as "the People of The Book." We are called that because we love to study the Bible, because we obey God's commandments in the Bible, and because we are the people about whom the Bible stories are told. Bible study is very important to us.

You may think of the Bible as one big book, but it is really a collection of many books. The Bible is divided into three main parts: the **Torah,** the **Prophets** (in Hebrew—**Nevi'im**) and the **Writings** (in Hebrew—**Ketuvim**). The first letters of the Hebrew names of each of the three main parts are combined to form the Hebrew word for the Bible— the **Tanakh.** (**T** is for Torah, **N** for Nevi'im, and **K** for Ketuvim.)

Ezekiel · Hosea · JOEL · AMOS · OBADIAH · JONAH · Micah · NAHUM · HABAKKUK · Zephaniah · HAGGAI · Zechariah · MALACHI · PSALMS · Proverbs · JOB · Song of Songs · RUTH · Lamentations · Ecclesiastes · ESTHER · Daniel · EZRA · NEHEMIAH · I Chronicles · II Chronicles

Do you know how many books are in the Hebrew Bible—the **Tanakh?** Count them to find out.

The first part of the Tanakh is the Torah. The word Torah means "teachings" or "law." The Torah is the Five Books of Moses. In English they are called **Genesis, Exodus, Leviticus, Numbers** and **Deuteronomy.**

The Torah begins at the very beginning, with God's creation of the world. The Torah contains stories we love to read. We read about Adam and Eve and about Noah and the great flood. We learn about the lives of Abraham, Isaac and Jacob and about Sarah, Rebeccah, Rachel and Leah. We read the stories of Joseph and his brothers and of Moses in the land of Egypt. These stories help us learn to be the kind of people we should be today.

We are not sure where Mount Sinai really is, but for hundreds of years people have come to this ragged mountaintop in the desert, believing that this is the place where Moses received the Ten Commandments.

God's laws and commandments are written in the Torah. The children of Israel received the Ten Commandments at Mount Sinai. Then Moses taught the children of Israel other Mitzvot that God wants us to do. For example, we must treat strangers kindly and help the poor. God's laws tell us how to observe Shabbat and the Jewish holidays—and they teach us how to live as a holy people.

The Ten Commandments

Challenge: Can you memorize the Ten Commandments?

1
I am God who brought you out of Egypt.

2
You must have no other gods besides me. You must not bow down to statues and call them gods.

3
You must not say the name God except at appropriate, important times.

4
Set aside the Sabbath day. Neither you, nor your animals, nor anyone who lives with you should do work on the Sabbath.

5
Honor your father and your mother.

6
You shall not murder.

7
You shall not take away another person's husband or wife.

8
You shall not steal.

9
You shall not tell lies about your neighbor.

10
You shall not want your neighbor's house or anything else that belongs to him.

When words are precious to us, we want to make them as beautiful as we can. This page from the Bible is illuminated. That means that an artist decorated the page with a painted design. If you look very closely you may be able to see that the shape of the flower petals in the center of the page is formed from tiny Hebrew letters. It took the artist three years to write and illuminate this Bible. He completed his work in Spain in 1483. Today, books are printed on presses, but fine artists still write Hebrew manuscripts by hand and illustrate them with beautiful illuminated designs.

The second part of the Tanakh is Nevi'im, the Prophets part. The Hebrew word for prophet is **navi.** It means "spokesperson," someone who speaks for God.

Each of the prophets was chosen to bring God's message to the people. The prophets reminded them to take care of hungry people and told them to be honest in business. The prophets scolded the people when they did not take care of widows and orphans. This made people feel guilty and angry. Sometimes they laughed at the prophets or ignored them altogether. Often the nevi'im were uncomfortable with their task. They did not want such a big responsibility. Sometimes the prophets argued with God about this.

The Words of the Prophets

The prophet Isaiah said, "This is what God wants: Stop doing evil. Learn to do good. Help those who have been wronged. Protect those who are helpless. Care for the orphan and the widow."

The prophet Amos said, "Hate the evil, and love the good, and establish justice in the gate."

The prophet Micah said, "God has told you what is good and what He wants of you: To do justice, to love goodness, and to walk with your God in a modest way."

Be A Prophet

The prophets lived long, long ago. Think about the world we live in today. Do you see injustices? Do you see people acting unfairly and dishonestly? How would you improve our world? Fill in the lines to let everyone know how you feel.

The third part of the Tanakh is Ketuvim, or Writings. The book of Psalms is one of the most famous books in Ketuvim. Psalms are religious poems. Each poem is numbered. There are 150 psalms in all, many of which are included in our prayer books. Part of the Book of Psalms was written by King David. David's 23rd Psalm is very well known. It begins, "The Lord is my shepherd, I shall not want." Do you know the next line?

The things we find buried from the past help us to understand the Bible better today. An archaeologist in Israel carefully brushes dirt away from pieces of pottery. The pieces are washed and labeled. If enough pieces are found, the pot may be put together like a puzzle. Then the archaelogists draw the pot's shape to learn more about it and the place it was found.

The Book of Proverbs is another well known book in the Ketuvim section of the Bible. A proverb is a little saying which describes a big idea.

Understanding Proverbs

Here are four proverbs. Pick one, and write what it means in your own words or draw a picture to illustrate the words. You can write a story to explain the proverb if you like.

Spare the rod and spoil the child.

Happy is the man who finds wisdom.

Do not quarrel with a man for no cause.

He who digs a pit will fall in it.

The Hebrew word **megillah** means "hand-written scroll." On Purim, the story of Queen Esther is read from a megillah. The scroll is kept in a case. The parchment is pulled from one end of the case as it is read and rolled back into the case when it is finished.

There are many books in Ketuvim.

The Book of Esther tells the story of Purim. The Songs of Songs is a long and beautiful poem about love. It is read in the synagogue on Passover, and parts of it are often read during wedding ceremonies. The saddest book in the Bible is also found in Ketuvim. It is known as the Book of Lamentations, and it mourns the destruction of Jerusalem.

Unscramble The Words

The words below are all names of books in our Bible. The letters in each name are correct, but some letters have changed places. Can you write each name correctly?

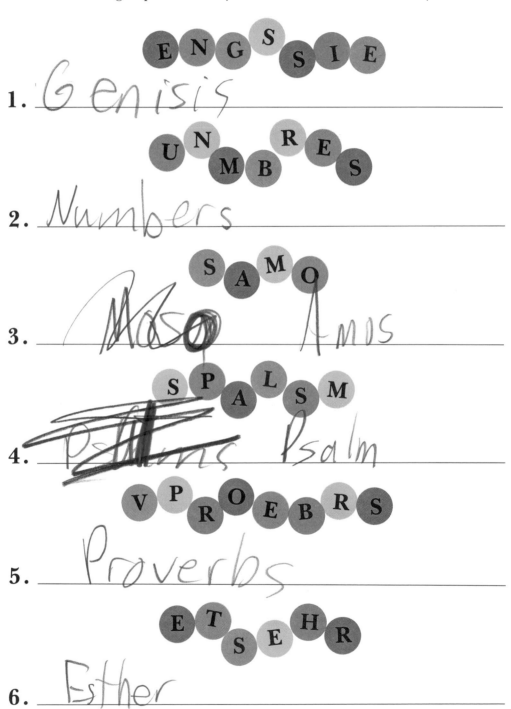

E N G S S I E

1. Genisis

U N M B R E S

2. Numbers

S A M O O

3. ~~Moso~~ Amos

S P A L S M

4. ~~Psalms~~ Psalm

V P R O E B R S

5. Proverbs

E T S E H R

6. Esther

Torah, Nevi'im and Ketuvim together make up the whole Hebrew Bible. Of these three parts, the Torah is the most important. In the next chapter you will learn why this is so, how the Torah is written and how it is read.

The Order Of The Books

Look at the Table of Contents and answer the questions.

TABLE OF CONTENTS
TANAKH

TORAH	PROPHETS		WRITINGS	
Genesis	Isaiah	Micah	Psalms	Esther
Exodus	Jeremiah	Nahum	Proverbs	Daniel
Leviticus	Ezekiel	Habakkuk	Job	Ezra
Numbers	Hosea	Zephaniah	Song of Songs	Nehemiah
Deuteronomy	Joel	Haggai	Ruth	Chronicles I
	Amos	Zechariah	Lamentations	Chronicles II
	Obadiah	Malachi	Ecclesiastes	
	Jonah			

The first book of Prophets is Isaiah. The last is Malachi. How many Prophets are there all together? _____

Which Prophet's name begins with O? _____

Three Prophets' names begin with H. Can you find them?

_____ _____ _____

What is the name of the fifth book in the Torah? _____

What book comes before Proverbs? _____

What is the name of the first book in the Bible? _____

What is the name of the last book in the Bible? _____

CHAPTER 10

The Sefer Torah

The Sefer Torah is the most important Jewish object. It is the first part of the Bible, and it contains the teachings our people live by.

We love and respect the Sefer Torah more than any other object, and so we have a special place to keep it. The Sefer Torah is kept in a wooden cabinet in the sanctuary of the synagogue called the Holy Ark or **Aron Hakodesh.** We face the Ark when we pray. To show our respect for the Torah, we all rise from our seats when the Ark is opened.

There stand the Torah scrolls. Each Torah is covered with a **mantle** or coat made of soft velvet or shiny satin. A silver breastplate may hang over the mantle. On top there may be a **keter**—a shining crown.

The Torah is precious to the
Jewish people, and we dress it
as beautifully as we can.

89

Sefer Torah is the Hebrew name for this "book," which is different from any other book you have seen. The word sefer means book, but in olden times books were not made like those we read today . . . and the Torah is a very old book! The Sefer Torah is not made of paper, and it does not have pages. It is written on a long, long scroll. The ends of the scroll are rolled around two wooden rollers. Each roller is called an etz ḥayim, which means tree of life. It is nice to think of the Torah as giving life to us.

Embroider A Mantle

Torah covers are often embroidered with Hebrew letters and designs. Connect the dots on the mantle and then color in the design.

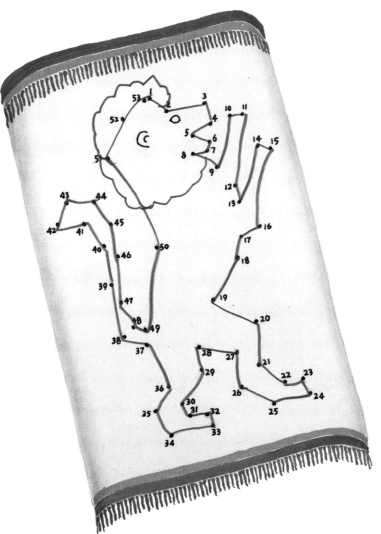

The ancient rabbis laid down very careful rules about how a Sefer Torah must be written. We still follow these rules today.

How a Sefer Torah is written

Only a very religious man called a **sofer,** or scribe, is allowed to write a Sefer Torah. He must copy his Torah so it looks *exactly* like every other Torah. The sofer sounds every letter and every word out loud before he writes it. The sofer must use a pen made from a feather dipped in special black ink. The ink contains ground up charcoal. The Torah is written on parchment. Parchment is made from sheep-skin or goatskin. When the writing is completed, the sofer sews all the sheets of parchment together, about 250 of them, and attaches the finished scroll to the wooden rollers. It can take a whole year to make a single copy of the Torah!

Sofer For A Day

There are many ways to write Hebrew letters, but a Torah scroll must be written with letters like these. Pretend that a black marker is a feather pen and carefully fill in each Hebrew letter. Remember, each letter in the Torah must be *perfect*.

The Torah is read in the synagogue. It is read aloud so that all of our people will know and remember what is written there. We make sure that we will never forget God's teachings. The congregation follows the readings from the Sefer Torah in a regular modern book that has the same words as the Torah scroll. This book is called the **Ḥumash.**

People from the congregation are called up to the Sefer Torah. Someone, like your older brother or sister, may be called. Because your brother goes *up* to the bimah this is known as an **aliyah** which means "going up." It is a great honor to be chosen. You will be called up to the Torah for the first time when you become a Bar or Bat Mitzvah.

The person called to the Torah recites two blessings. One blessing is chanted before the Torah is read. When the Torah reading is completed, another blessing is recited.

After the Torah reading is completed, the scroll is lifted high in the air and turned to face the congregation. The person who raised the Torah then sits on a chair and holds the scroll upright. A second person rolls the scroll together and dresses the Torah. Just as it is an honor to recite the Torah blessings, so it is an honor to lift and dress the Torah.

Suppose your older sister is reading from the Torah. Her hands may be sweaty, and she might accidently smear the ink or soil the parchment while she is reading—so every reader uses a pointer. This pointer is called a **yad,** which is the Hebrew word for hand. We use the yad to show our respect for God's words by not directly touching the Torah.

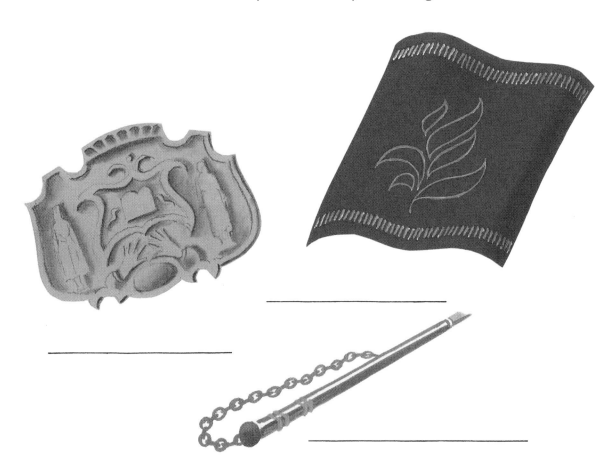

Dressing The Torah

Here are drawings of the items we use to dress the Sefer Torah before we return it to the Aron HaKodesh. Write the name of each item under the drawing, and then number the items in the order by which you would dress the Torah.

It is a very joyous time when a new Sefer Torah is brought to the synagogue. The scroll is carried into the building under a canopy, like the covering the bride and groom stand under during the wedding ceremony. There is dancing and a celebration like the one on Simḥat Torah.

It takes one full year to read the whole Torah. We read one specific portion each Shabbat. This is called the portion of the week or **parshat hashavua.** In some synagogues, it takes three years to complete the whole reading. Those synagogues read shorter portions each week. We also read from the Torah on the Jewish holidays. There are Torah portions for Passover and Yom Kippur, for Rosh Hashanah and Ḥanukkah. We read from the Torah at the beginning of each month, on Rosh Hodesh, when the new moon is a small sliver in the sky. And, of course, YOU will read from the Torah on your Bar or Bat Mitzvah day.

True or False

Put a T next to a true statement.
Put an F next to an untrue statement.

1. _____
The sofer can use a ballpoint pen to write a Torah.

2. _____
The sofer sounds each word out loud as he writes it.

3. _____
The special paper a sofer writes on is called vellum.

4. _____
The Torah is kept in a special cabinet in the sanctuary called Aron Hakodesh.

5. _____
A breastplate hangs over the Torah mantle.

6. _____
A keter is the pointer used to keep our place in the Torah.

7. _____
The Sefer Torah has pages and a cover like a textbook.

8. _____
A yad is a pointer.

9. _____
When you are called to the Torah, you are being honored with an aliyah.

10. _____
The Torah portion we read each Shabbat is called parshat hashavua.

96

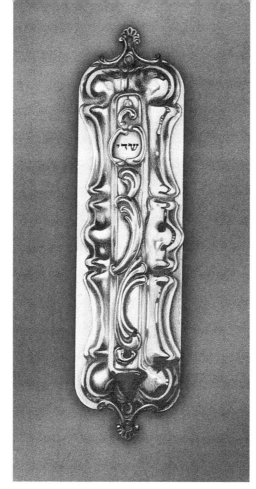

The Hebrew word **Shaddai** appears on every mezuzah parchment. It is a name for God meaning "Almighty." This mezuzah case has an opening through which the word can be seen on the parchment.

11 Objects At Home

Your home is a warm and safe place. You know that you belong there, no matter what. Your home is a Jewish place. Look around and you will find many objects which help make your home a Jewish one.

Begin your search outside. Look at the front door of your house. There you may see a little container on the right side of the door. It is called a **mezuzah.** Mezuzah is actually the Hebrew word for "doorpost." When we hang a mezuzah we mark our house as a Jewish home where people follow God's laws.

97

The mezuzah case at your front door might be made of brass. Perhaps your friend's mezuzah case is made of silver or wood. Yet every mezuzah is the same in one way. Each mezuzah contains a piece of parchment rolled up inside. On the parchment, a sofer has written 22 lines in Hebrew. These include the first two paragraphs of the Shema. These passages from the Torah instruct us to love God, to teach God's commandments and to attach God's words to our doorposts.

How do we hang the mezuzah?

The mezuzah is attached to the doorpost on the right side as you enter the house or room. It hangs no more than one-third of the way down from the top of the doorpost. It is the custom to slant the top of the mezuzah toward the inside of the house or into the room. Before hanging the mezuzah, we recite two blessings. The first one reminds us that God commanded us to hang the mezuzah. In the second blessing we thank God for keeping us alive and well to perform this Mitzvah.

Each mezuzah case looks different. One is made of wood and another of colored plastic. A mezuzah case may be made of brass or have an interesting shape. Yet each mezuzah is the same in one very important way. Every mezuzah contains the same Hebrew words written on a piece of parchment.

Mezuzah Maze

In olden times, traveling was difficult and even dangerous. People went on foot or on horseback from one town to another. A mezuzah on the doorpost was a welcome sign to Jewish travelers. It marked a Jewish home where a stranger could find a kosher meal and a bed for the night. Help this traveler find the way.

בָּרוּךְ אַתָּה יְיָ אֱלֹהֵינוּ מֶלֶךְ הָעוֹלָם
הַמּוֹצִיא לֶחֶם מִן הָאָרֶץ.

Baruch atah adonai elohenu melech ha-olam ha-motzi leḥem min ha-aretz.

Blessed are You, Lord our God, Ruler of the universe, who brings forth bread from the earth.

You can continue your search for Jewish objects inside your house. You will probably find candlesticks used for holding the Sabbath and holiday candles. On Friday night just before sundown, we light the Shabbat candles and recite a blessing. As you look around the dinner table at your family, you forget about fighting with your brother after school, or arguing with your little sister about sharing your bike. As the Shabbat candles slowly burn, you feel good because you are all together as a family.

On the Shabbat table there is a cup for wine. It is often made of silver. As the family sits down to dinner, we recite a blessing called **kiddush** over the wine. The braided **ḥallah** bread is covered with a cloth. Sometimes it has the words Shabbat Shalom—Sabbath peace—embroidered on it.

בָּרוּךְ אַתָּה יְיָ אֱלֹהֵינוּ מֶלֶךְ הָעוֹלָם

בּוֹרֵא פְּרִי הַגָּפֶן.

Baruch atah adonai elohenu melech ha-olam boray p'ri ha-gafen.

Blessed are You, Lord our God, Ruler of the universe, who creates the fruit of the vine.

Embroider The Ḥallah Cover

Connect the dots on the ḥallah cover and then color in the design.

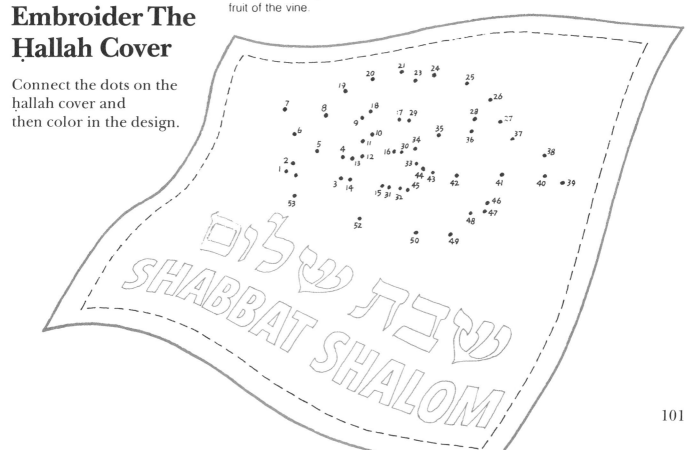

As you face the ḥanukkiah, place the first candle on your right. New candles are added to the left. The new candle is always lit first.

Almost every Jewish family has a Ḥanukkah menorah called a **ḥanukkiah.** The ḥanukkiah is lit on the eight nights of Ḥanukkah. There are nine places for candles, one place for each night and the ninth place reserved for the **shamash** or helper candle. We use the shamash to light the other candles. On the first night of Ḥanukkah we light one candle. On each night we add another candle until the ḥanukkiah is filled. The candles burn brightly in the window while the family plays Ḥanukkah games. Do you have a **dreidel**—a Ḥanukkah top—in your house?

The objects on the Passover table help us to retell the story of Moses and to remember how God brought us out of Egypt.

Some things are used only once a year, on Passover.

The seder plate holds the special foods we use to tell the Passover story. There is a place for a roasted egg, parsley and three other things. Do you know what they are? You can find the answer in the **Haggadah,** the book we read at the Passover **seder.** Perhaps your grandfather will explain the symbols to you at your family seder. A wine cup is placed on the seder table for Elijah the Prophet. Do you have a **Cup of Elijah** in your cupboard? Does your grandmother or great-grandmother have one in hers?

How Many Objects Do You Know?

Unscramble the word below each picture.

REEDS TELAP

PCU FO HELIAJ

HAZZUME

DIRSUD

BAHBATS SLEDNAC

LAIGLEMH

GAAGAHDH

KATNAH

HUDKIDS PCU

LIREEDD

KUHHNAIK

The bookcase is a good place to continue your search for Jewish objects in your home. Can you find a **Siddur,** a Jewish prayerbook? Look for a Tanakh, our Hebrew Bible. It may be printed all in Hebrew or with English translation too. Some of the Jewish books you find may be old and musty. Others may be brand new. Books make your home a place for Jewish study.

Look carefully at the photograph these people are holding. It is a picture of them when they were young. Photographs can help us remember our past. Do your grandparents have pictures of themselves when they were younger?

How about things that hang on the walls or are stored away in the attic? You may see photographs of your great–great–grandparents. Maybe your mother has saved old letters written by your relatives long ago on crumbling paper. How do you feel when you look in a picture album at a fuzzy photograph of your great–grandfather dressed in old-fashioned clothes?

All of these objects are an important part of a Jewish home. We use them to celebrate our holidays, and they help us to remember our past. But things alone to not make a home Jewish. None of them matter as much as the people do. It is your family that makes your home the loving Jewish place it is.

Hidden Pictures

How many Jewish objects can you find hidden
in the picture below?

12

Jewish Food

Food is a gift from God. All animals and all people eat food, but only people eat "meals." A meal is a ceremony, so we wash our hands before sitting down at the table. We think of God whenever we eat, so before we eat we recite a blessing as a way of saying thank you to God. We invite friends and family as well as the poor and the homeless to share our meals. Hospitality is a commandment, a Mitzvah.

Some foods are particularly important to Jewish people. We especially enjoy the foods we eat at our holiday celebrations. These foods are symbols. They remind us of important ideas when we eat them. What is sweet about Purim? What is crispy about Ḥanukkah? What is bitter about Passover? You will learn the answers in this chapter.

We enjoy eating crispy brown potato pancakes on Ḥanukkah. These are called **latkes.** Some people celebrate Ḥanukkah by eating jelly doughnuts. Both of these holiday treats are fried in oil. Why do we eat them on Ḥanukkah? In the Ḥanukkah story, we learn that when the Maccabees entered the Temple in Jerusalem, they found only one small bottle of oil, enough to burn for only one night. But something wonderful happened. The oil lasted not for one night, but for eight! To remember this miracle, we light candles or oil lamps for the eight nights of Ḥanukkah and we eat foods fried in oil.

We celebrate the miracle of Ḥanukkah by eating potato pancakes fried in oil. Grating the potatoes is the most difficult part of the recipe. Do you know why we eat food fried in oil on Ḥanukkah?

Latkes Recipe

 4 large potatoes

1 teaspoon salt

2 eggs

3 tablespoons flour

1/2 teaspoon baking powder

 vegetable oil for frying

1
Wash, peel and grate the potatoes.

2
Drain off the liquid.

3
Beat the eggs.

4
Mix everything together, except the oil.

5
Heat the oil in a skillet pan.

6
Drop the mixture by tablespoons into the hot oil.

7
Fry the latkes on both sides until brown.

8
Drain the latkes on paper towels.

9
Serve the latkes with applesauce or sour cream.

On Rosh Hashanah we dip ḥallah and apples into honey because we hope the new year will be sweet. The ḥallah's round shape reminds us that one year is over and a new one is beginning. We have come around in a circle.

On Purim we eat delicious cakes filled with poppy-seeds or fruit. They are called **hamantashen.** Each cake is shaped like a triangle. Why do hamantashen have three sides? Some people say the sides help us remember evil Haman's three-cornered hat. Others say they remind us of Haman's pointy ears. We don't really know if Haman wore such a hat, and we might not always think of the shape of Haman's ears when we eat Purim cakes . . . but we do know how tasty hamantashen are, and how nice the house smells while they are baking! Those good things help us to remember brave Queen Esther and how she saved our people in Shushan long ago.

111

The hamantashen cookie dough is cut into circles and poppyseeds or fruit are spooned into the center. Three sides of the circle are then pinched together to form a triangle. What is your favorite hamantashen filling?

Different blessings for different foods.

The blessing we say before a meal is called **hamotzi.** It is actually recited over bread, but it is for everything we will eat except wine and fresh fruit. The blessing over wine is called **kiddush.** There are many other blessings too, such as the one recited before eating fruits that grow on trees, like apples, and oranges. There is a blessing for eating "fruits of the earth," such as tomatoes, carrots, corn and bananas. Grains other than bread also have their own blessing. Meat, fish and eggs have still another. The blessing we recite after finishing a meal is called **Birkhat Hamazon.**

Which Blessing To Say?

Each blessing begins with these 6 words:
YOU ARE BLESSED, LORD OUR GOD, RULER OF THE WORLD

Then another line is added:

WHO BRINGS FORTH BREAD FROM THE EARTH.

WHO CREATES THE FRUIT OF THE VINE.

WHO CREATES THE FRUIT OF THE TREE.

WHO CREATES THE FRUIT OF THE EARTH.

BY WHOSE WORD ALL THINGS COME INTO BEING.

Can you connect each blessing to the correct food?

On Passover, we eat **matzah**—hard, flat bread. Why do we do this? When a baker makes bread yeast or some other kind of leavening is mixed into the dough. This makes the bread rise up and become soft and fluffy when it is baked. It takes time for the dough to rise. On Passover we celebrate the exodus from the land of Egypt. When our ancestors left Egypt, they were in a great hurry. There was no time to wait for the dough to rise to become fluffy bread, so they quickly made unleavened bread. It was hard and flat. Matzah reminds us of those long ago days.

A plate on the seder table holds five foods that remind us of important things. A roasted lamb bone **(zeroa)** reminds us of the ancient sacrifices in the Temple. A roasted egg **(betzah)** reminds us of the new life that comes each spring. A bitter herb

As we begin the seder we say, "Let all who are hungry come and eat." Passover is a time for sharing. That is why we invite guests to share our seder meal.

114

such as horseradish **(maror)** helps us remember the bitter taste of slavery. **Ḥaroset** (a mixture of chopped apples, nuts and wine) looks like the cement that held together the bricks made by the Jewish slaves in Egypt. When we dip the green vegetable **(karpas)** into salt water, we remember the tears our ancestors cried when they were slaves. We taste the bitter maror and enjoy the sweet ḥaroset, but we do not eat the zeroa or the betzah. They are just symbols to help us remember.

Fill The Seder Plate

Label each food on the seder plate. On the second line, write what each one helps us to remember.

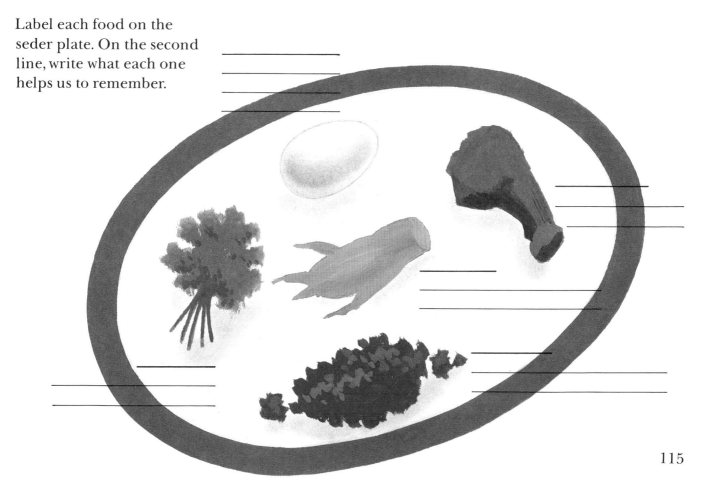

The Dietary Laws

There is a Hebrew word that describes how some Jews eat every day. The word is **kosher** and it means fit or proper. In the Torah there are many rules about the kinds of foods Jews may or may not eat. The only animals that may be eaten are those like the cow and the sheep and birds like the chicken and turkey. All vegetables and plants may be eaten. Fish must have fins and scales. There are also rules about how foods may be prepared. Meat is not cooked or eaten with milk. Together, all these rules are called dietary laws. Jews who follow these laws are said to keep kosher.

Many Jewish foods are enjoyed by all kinds of people. Do you like to eat bagels and lox, pastrami on rye, ḥallah, gefilte fish, blintzes and knishes? Originally these foods came from different countries, but now they are American favorites. Some Israeli foods, like falafel and pita bread, are also very popular. When we eat these foods we have a strong feeling of being part of the Jewish community today. When we thank God for our food, we feel a strong connection with our ancestors who lived long ago.

Look carefully at these packages. Can you find the symbols that tell us these foods are kosher?

Design A Billboard

Large billboards on highways advertise many products. Use the one below to show a Jewish holiday food. You can write words and draw pictures too. Will you sell matzah for Passover, latkes for Ḥanukkah, hamantashen for Purim or honey for Rosh Hashanah?

119

CHAPTER 13

How We Pray

When we pray, we are talking to God. In some prayers, we ask God for help. If your uncle is sick, you pray that he will soon be well again. Sometimes we pray because we are sad or frightened. Talking to God makes us feel stronger. In some prayers we ask God to forgive us. If you did something you are sorry about, asking for God's forgiveness can help you do better next time. In some prayers we thank God for the many good things we have. We all find our own personal ways to pray.

Jewish people have been praying to God for a long, long time. Some of our prayers are very, very old, and Jewish people said them hundreds—even thousands—of years ago. Jewish prayers tell about the things that our people believe in and the ideas that have kept our people together and have kept our people strong.

Praying together in the synagogue helps us to remember that we belong to one people. Lighting the holiday candles together at home helps us to remember that we belong to one family.

Jewish people pray together in the synagogue. We have set times for our services and certain ways of saying our prayers. We use a special prayerbook. The Hebrew word for prayerbook is **siddur** which means order. The siddur contains blessings, prayers, and poems called psalms. All these are arranged in a definite order so that everybody in the synagogue can follow the rabbi and sing along with the cantor. When we use the words of the siddur we are all able to pray together as part of one congregation.

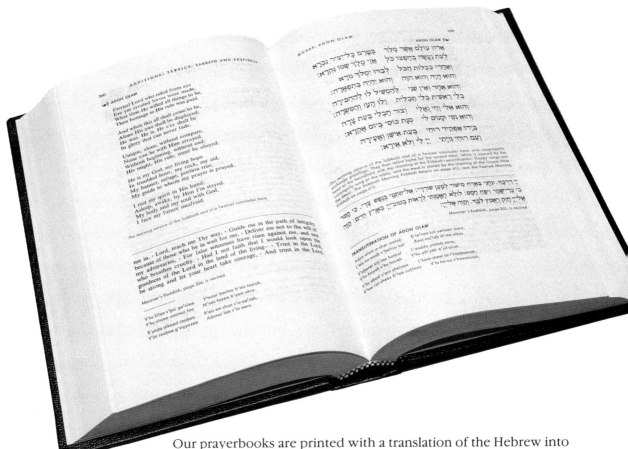

Our prayerbooks are printed with a translation of the Hebrew into English, our everyday language. When we understand what we are saying, we can pray with all our hearts, with kavanah. Do you recognize the prayer in this photograph? We sing it at the end of synagogue services.

Table Of Contents

The siddur contains prayers we say in the synagogue and prayers we recite at home. Can you find the correct pages to answer the questions below?

SIDDUR
TABLE OF CONTENTS

We are ready to take out the Torah from the Aron Hakodesh. Turn to page _____ .

We will shake the lulav. Turn to page _____ .

We have finished the meal and will recite the blessing. Turn to page _____ .

We will bless the wine. Turn to page _____ .

It is Friday evening in the synagogue. Turn to page _____ .

We will celebrate the Maccabees' victory. Turn to page _____ .

Long ago, our rabbis decided that ten Jewish men over the age of Bar Mitzvah were needed to form an official congregation. We call these ten Jews a **minyan.** Ten Jews must be present to read the Torah during a prayer service. Certain prayers, like the Mourner's Kaddish, are not said without a minyan. In days past, women were not counted as part of the ten. Today, most Conservative and all Reform congregations do count women over the age of Bat Mitzvah as part of the minyan needed to make a praying congregation.

The **shofar** is made from the horn of a male sheep, a ram. It makes a strange sharp sound when it is blown. In ancient times, the shofar was blown at important times. It was blown at Mount Sinai, when the Jewish people promised to obey God's Torah. The sound of the shofar told the people when a new month was beginning. The sound of the shofar called everyone to hear important news. You will hear the shofar in the synagogue on the High Holy Days. Its sound reminds us of things that happened long ago.

Celebrating special days calls for special prayers. Most of our holidays have their own prayers, and these are found in the siddur. There are so many changes and additions in the Rosh Hashanah and Yom Kippur prayer services, that we need a prayerbook just for the High Holy Days. This prayerbook is called a **maḥzor.**

One of the most important prayers in every service is the **Shema.** In English we say: "Hear, O Israel, the Lord is our God, the Lord is One." In Hebrew we say: "Shema Yisrael, Adonay Elohenu, Adonay Eḥad." This is followed by three paragraphs from the Torah, completing the Shema. The Shema tells us to love and obey God and to follow God's commandments, the Mitzvot.

Shema Yisrael

As you fill in the words of the Shema, think about what they mean. As you work, try to memorize the prayer.

שְׁמַע יִשְׂרָאֵל יְהוָה
אֱלֹהֵינוּ יְהוָה
אֶחָד׃

HEAR, O ISRAEL, THE LORD
IS OUR GOD, THE LORD IS ONE.

This child is learning to recite the **Shema.** When we hold our hands over our eyes it helps us to concentrate with all our might.

Prayer reminds us that the world can be a better place. We believe that each of us has a responsibility to make that happen, but without study, we cannot know what we can do. Only through study do we learn what God requires of us. The first line of the Shema and the paragraphs following it are taken from the Torah. When we say the Shema we are really studying the Bible. Of course, the most important kind of prayer-study is the reading of the Torah itself. Most of our prayers are the same words and sentences that our grandfathers and great–grandmothers said. Did you know that the six main words of the Shema were spoken in the desert when Moses led the people of Israel? Prayer connects us to the whole history of our people. Not only the words of the prayers, but the language of our prayers connects us too. We use Hebrew in our prayer services. Praying in Hebrew reminds us that we are one people, with a common language, all praying for the same things.

Good Things, Bad Things

Studying the Bible guides us to lead good lives—lives that will help other people. In the spaces on the left, list some things that God wants us to do. On the right side, list some of the things God tells us not to do.

THINGS WE SHOULD DO

THINGS WE SHOULD NOT DO

You can go to a Jewish prayer service anywhere in the world and hear most of the prayers being recited in Hebrew. These Jews live in Djerba, a city in Tunisia. If you could hear their prayers, you would find that they are very much like the ones you say in your synagogue back home. Hebrew prayer binds our people together.

Some of our prayers are in Aramaic, a language that was spoken by Jews in Babylonia 2,000 years ago—much the same way we now speak English. The **Kaddish** prayer, recited several times during our service, is mostly in Aramaic. It looks like Hebrew and uses the same alphabet. If you can read Hebrew, you can read Aramaic too!

How some Jews dress to pray.

Some Jews wear a **kippah** when they pray, which is a small, round cap worn at the back of the head. In Yiddish it is called a **yarmulke.** A **tallit** is a prayer shawl worn around a Jew's shoulders. It is usually white with blue or black stripes. **Tefillin** are two little black leather boxes. One box is strapped to the head and the other to the arm during weekday morning services. Inside each box are verses from the Torah written on parchment, like the contents of a mezuzah. In the past, a kippah, a tallit and tefillin were worn only by men. Today, some women wear them too.

The fringes on the bottom of a **tallit** are called **tzizit.** Tzizit are made of white threads knotted in a special way.

When people use their bodies as well as their thoughts, it helps them to pray with kavanah. Some Jews sway back and forth as they pray. To help you concentrate with all your might, you can hold your hands over your eyes and close them tightly when you say the Shema. Jews who wear a tallit touch or kiss the fringes when they read the commandments in the Shema. We all bend our knees and bow our heads during the Alenu prayer near the end of services.

Jewish prayers help us to walk with God and lead us to do the right things. Prayers teach us to be kind to one another. Praying can help you become the kind of person who wants to do something to make the world a better place for all people everywhere.

A Minyan Of Words

Look across and down to find the 10 hidden words. Circle each one as you find it. When you find all 10 you will have a minyan of words.

B	L	W	K	I	P	P	A	H	G	K
C	D	T	A	L	L	I	T	M	M	A
S	I	D	D	U	R	F	P	N	I	V
H	A	B	D	P	R	A	Y	T	T	A
E	R	M	I	N	Y	A	N	Z	Z	N
M	A	I	S	B	A	J	Q	I	V	A
A	M	A	H	Z	O	R	H	Z	O	H
X	A	T	E	F	I	L	T	U	T	M

CHALLENGE: Can you write the meaning of each word you found?

WORD

MEANING

129

CHAPTER 14

How We Celebrate

Pretend that today is your birthday. To everyone else it is just another day, but to you today is very important! It is a time to celebrate.

At your birthday celebration you play games and eat ice cream and cake—but first, you blow out the candles while your family and friends sing "Happy Birthday to You." Three things make your party a celebration: There is food. There is family. And there is a ceremony.

A Jewish celebration is a kind of party too. These same three things are present. Since it is a happy time, there is a feast. Sometimes the food is special for the day, like the latkes on Ḥanukkah and the blintzes on Shavuot. We eat together with our family. The ceremony is always special for the day. We read the Megillah on Purim. We light the candles for eight nights on Ḥanukkah. Our celebrations connect us to God and to our people.

When we eat in the sukkah, we remember our ancestors who traveled through the desert. We feel grateful that God brought them to the land of Israel where they could settle and grow. We think of the hard work they did, farming and harvesting, and feel the happiness and holiday excitement that they felt when their work was done.

Jews celebrate holidays about events in our history. We also celebrate important events in our own lives. When a child is born the cycle of life begins. The baby is made a member of the Jewish people. Babies may be named at a celebration in the synagogue and often their parents have a **Brit** which is celebrated at home. On the eighth day after birth, Jewish boys are circumcised during the Brit Milah ceremony. These celebrations are signs of the agreement, or covenant, between God and the Jewish people. Brit means covenant.

131

The Sheheḥeyanu Blessing

Sometimes we celebrate in the synagogue, and at other times we celebrate at home—but we always thank God for making our celebrations possible. In our joy, we often recite the **Sheheḥeyanu** blessing. Your parents will probably recite Sheheḥeyanu at your Bar or Bat Mitzvah. We all recite the blessing on the first night of Ḥanukkah. The Sheheḥeyanu blessing is an important one to know.

Your first name is a gift from your parents. Your second name is your family's name. The most important thing is what we do with our names. We bring honor to the name our parents gave us by making it a good name, a **shem tov,** by the way we spend our time and live our lives.

Learn The Blessing

בָּרוּךְ אַתָּה יְיָ אֱלֹהֵינוּ מֶלֶךְ הָעוֹלָם
שֶׁהֶחֱיָנוּ וְקִיְּמָנוּ וְהִגִּיעָנוּ לַזְּמַן הַזֶּה.

Baruch atah adonai elohenu melech ha-olam sheheheyanu
v'kiyemanu v'hi-gi-anu lazman ha-zeh.

Blessed are You, Lord our God, Ruler of the Universe,
who has kept us alive and strong and brought us to this
season.

Important moments in your life as a student are shared with God and with the Jewish community. Jews are proud and happy when their children begin to learn. It is something to celebrate. The first celebration comes when children start religious school. In some synagogues, there is a consecration service. There is a bigger celebration when students finish a period of Jewish learning—at the age of Bar or Bat Mitzvah. At that time, students become full members of the Jewish community and are expected to begin observing Mitzvot on their own. Every time we finish studying a book of the Bible or Talmud, Jewish tradition encourages a celebration which is called a **siyyum.** And in some synagogues, when students are 15 or 16 years old, they are confirmed as they graduate from religious school. This is time for another celebration.

The **ḥuppah,** a wedding canopy, is made of silk or some other material hung like a small ceiling from four poles. During the wedding ceremony, the bride and groom stand together under the canopy. It is nice to think of the ḥuppah as a symbol of God's covering protection.

Marriage is important to the Jewish people, and a wedding is a time of great celebration. When two people marry they become part of each other. Together they will create children and a family. The bride and groom stand together under a ḥuppah, a wedding canopy, where the wedding ring is given and the marriage contract is read. The wedding feast follows, with music and dancing and the giving of gifts.

The Jewish year is full of holidays. There are happy noisy times like Simḥat Torah and Ḥanukkah. There are quiet, serious times like Yom Kippur and Tisha B'Av, a day to remember the destruction of the Temple in Jerusalem. There are Rosh Hashanah cards to send and Purim costumes to sew. There is a sukkah to build in the fall and a Passover seder to prepare in the spring.

Holiday Want Ads

In the newspaper below you will find ads placed by people looking for holiday jobs. On the line under each advertisement, write the name of the correct holiday.

It's all in the wrist! Expert spinner will teach you the winning twist.

_____

Sweet tooth? Hire me and taste the best three-cornered cakes ever!

_____

Shammash. Will light your fire for eight nights.

_____

Decorator. Outdoor constructions using corn stalks and vegetables.

_____

Baker. Specializing in creamy cheese cake.

_____

Afikoman Hider. There's no such thing as an easy hiding place when you hire this matzah magician.

_____

Expert shofar blower makes outstanding blast.

_____

Most holidays come once each year, but one of our most important holidays comes every week. On Friday evening as the sun sets, Shabbat begins. We light the Sabbath candles and recite the kiddush over wine. On Friday night Jews often invite a guest to dinner. It is nice to share our festive meal with others. On Saturday morning many families go to the synagogue. Sometimes children attend Sabbath school or special children's services while their parents attend prayer services in the main sanctuary. Shabbat celebrates the seventh day of creation. Just as God rested after making the world, so Shabbat is a day of rest for us. It is a day of celebration, and as on all Jewish celebrations, there is food and family and ceremony.

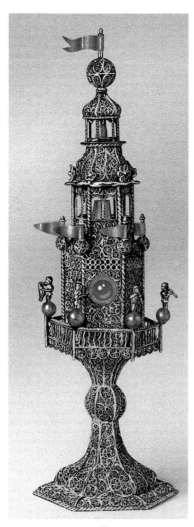

Sweet-smelling spices are kept in a **Havdalah** spice box. It is often made of silver and shaped like a castle tower.

What is Havdalah?

When three stars appear in the Saturday night sky, Shabbat has ended. We then have a ceremony called **Havdalah.** Havdalah means separation. We light a Havdalah candle. It is braided and is often very colorful. Blessings are said over a cup of wine and over sweet-smelling spices. We all smell the cloves and cinnamon because we hope the sweetness of Shabbat will last all week long. Shabbat is now over, and a new week has begun. We wish each other a "good week"—**"Shavua Tov."**

Holiday Customs

The holidays are celebrated a little differently in every Jewish home. Describe how your family celebrates by answering the questions below.

Are Shabbat candles lit in your home? _____

Who recites the blessing? _____

Have you ever seen a Havdalah ceremony? _____

Does your family eat any special foods on Shabbat? _____

What are they? _____

Are there any special activities that your family does together on Shabbat? _____

Is there anything your family does not do on Shabbat? _____

Do you exchange gifts on Hanukkah? _____

Do you attend Rosh Hashanah synagogue services for one day or for two? _____

Do you build a sukkah? Where? _____

Do you dress in a costume on Purim? _____

Does your family mail Rosh Hashanah greeting cards? _____

Which new holiday customs would you like to follow in the future? _____

We celebrate a birthday with a birthday party. We celebrate the birthday of the world on Rosh Hashanah. We celebrate the beginning of understanding the Torah with a Bar or Bat Mitzvah. We celebrate God's giving the Torah on Shavuot. All through the Jewish year, and all through a Jewish lifetime, our celebrations mark important events.

ACROSS

1. At every celebration there is food, family and a _____ .

2. We light the Ḥanukkah candles for _____ nights.

3. When Shabbat has ended, we have a ceremony called _____ .

4. At the Passover _____ we tell the story of the exodus from Egypt.

5. The holiday we celebrate most often is _____ .

6. We read the Megillah on _____ .

7. We celebrate God's giving the Torah on _____ .

8. We shake the lulav on the holiday of _____ .

9. Jewish holidays come throughout the _____ .

DOWN

1. We __ __ __ __ __ __ __ __ __ !

A Crossword Puzzle

How do we mark an important event?
To find the answer, fill in the words across.
The answer is 1-down.

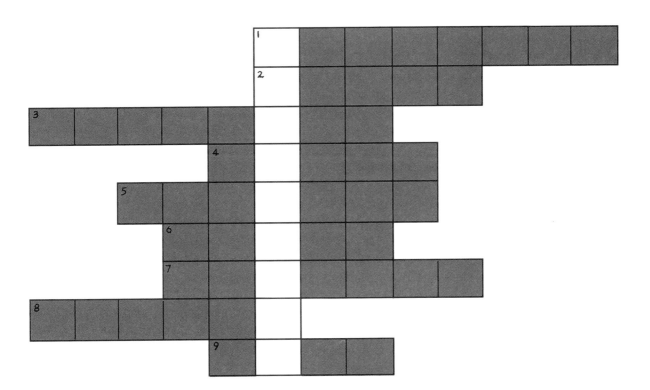

CHAPTER 15

How We Remember

Jewish people do a lot of remembering.

Each spring when we read from the Haggadah at the Passover seder, we remember how God freed us from slavery in Egypt. When we spin our graggers and eat hamantashen on Purim, we remember Queen Esther's bravery. Every time we read from the Torah we remember God's commandments, given to us so long ago. Jewish people have a long history, and we have a great deal to remember.

We have special ways of remembering people who are no longer with us. Our Jewish customs and ceremonies teach us what to do when someone dies. It is very hard to lose someone we love. Our tradition shows us that love continues even after death.

Death comes to all things that live. When a flower dies, its seeds make new flowers grow.

Our rabbis said it would be wise to celebrate a returning ship, for it has come home safely to port. How is it the same with people?

When someone dies, the funeral takes place as soon as possible. Jews are usually buried the day after death. In this way family and friends can gather together quickly to give love and support to the people who are in mourning.

First the service is held in a funeral home or sometimes in the synagogue. The funeral service is not long. A few psalms and prayers are recited. Then we hear a short speech about the person who has died. It is called a eulogy. Usually the rabbi gives the eulogy. Sometimes a relative will speak. Eulogies are not always sad. Some stories about the person's life can make us smile.

We celebrate a person's life

Our rabbis taught that when we think about death, we should imagine two boats in a harbor. One is leaving port. The other is returning. People usually celebrate the ship that is going away. They ignore the one that has sailed safely back to port. But the ship that is leaving must face the dangers of an ocean voyage. It would be wise, the rabbis said, to celebrate the returning ship, for it has come home safely. It is the same with people. When a person is born, no one knows whether life will be good or bad, easy or difficult. But when people end their lives with good names, having lived successful lives, that is a time to rejoice as well as to mourn.

How do you feel about this idea?

Find The Meaning

When someone dies, there is something we do. To find the word, fill in each square that has a blue dot in it.

Use the hidden word to complete each of these sentences.

On Passover we _____ how God freed us from slavery.

On Purim we _____ Queen Esther's bravery.

When we read from the Torah, we _____ God's commandments.

When people die we _____ them.

Sometimes the garment worn by each member of the family is cut or torn. This custom is very old. It comes from Bible times, when clothes were torn to show sadness. The cut is often made in a piece of black ribbon pinned to the mourners' clothing. The ribbon may be worn for 30 days. If you see a person wearing this ribbon, you know that someone they love has recently died.

After the funeral service, the family goes to the cemetery where many other Jewish people are buried. The coffin is lowered into the ground. The traditional Jewish coffin is a simple wooden box put together without nails. The Mourner's Kaddish is recited for the person who has died. This same prayer has been said for 2,000 years.

At home, friends have prepared supper. The door is open. A neighbor carries in a pot of home-made soup. Bringing food after a funeral is a Jewish custom. It makes the mourners feel less lonely. They know that they have loving friends.

143

Do You Know Why?

Explain the reason for each of the following customs.

1. When someone dies the funeral takes place as soon as possible.

_____

2. Clothing or a ribbon is cut.

_____

3. Friends prepare supper.

_____

As you read on, find the reasons for these customs.

4. A stone is placed on the grave.

_____

5. The mourners stay home for seven days.

_____

6. A **yahrzeit** candle is lit on the anniversary of a person's death.

_____

7. Money is donated to worthy causes in the name of the person who has died.

_____

This Jewish cemetery is in the Soviet Union. If you look closely at the tombstones, you will see the pictures of the people who are buried there.

144

The Shivah Period

The first seven days after the funeral is called **shivah.** Shivah means seven. It is a period of time set aside for remembering the person who has died. The mourners do not go to work or to school. They stay at home. They sit on low stools or boxes instead of chairs. Friends and relatives come to visit and comfort them. Prayer services are held.

The **yahrzeit** candle burns for 24 hours. It is lit on the evening before the anniversary of a person's death.

When the shivah period is over, the mourners return to their regular schedule—but the person who died is not forgotten. In some communities, special observances continue for 30 more days. This period is called **Shloshim,** which means 30. Every year on the anniversary of a person's death, we light a **yahrzeit** candle at home. This is the Jewish way of remembering and honoring that person. In the synagogue it is customary to read aloud the names of people whose death anniversary—yahrzeit—is being remembered. The Mourner's Kaddish is recited by members of the family.

145

Another way of remembering is by giving money to worthy causes in the names of people who have died. By giving Tzedakah, doing a Mitzvah in their names, we honor their memories. When we help people in the world today, we honor the memory of all Jewish people throughout history.

Planting a tree in Israel is a thoughtful way of remembering a person who has died.

Trees have been Planted in Israel

on the land of the Jewish National Fund

in loving memory of:

1 TREE

And Eternal Life He Has Planted in Our Midst

וְחַיֵּי עוֹלָם נָטַע בְּתוֹכֵנוּ

Looking For Understanding

After death, what happens to love:
To find the answer, fill in the words across.
The answer is 1–down.

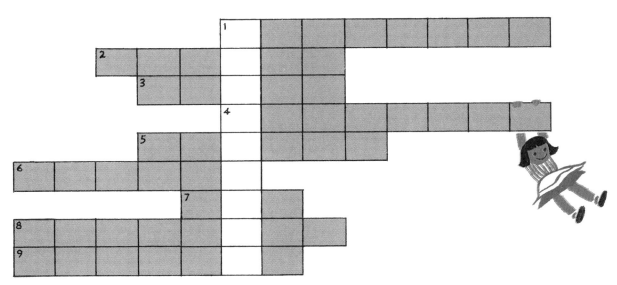

ACROSS

1. People are buried in a place called a _____.

2. The short speech about the person who died is called a _____.

3. We give _____ to worthy causes to honor the memory of a person who has died.

4. In Hebrew this is called _____.

5. The first seven days after the funeral is called _____.

6. A wooden box put together without nails is called a _____.

7. A piece of ribbon pinned on a mourner's clothes is _____.

8. On the anniversary of a person's death, a _____ candle is lit.

9. The prayer recited for the person who has died is called Mourner's _____.

DOWN

1. Even after death, love __ __ __ __ __ __ __ __ __.

147

16

Our Jewish Year

How do we know when to celebrate Rosh Hashanah? How do we know the date to light a yahrzeit candle to remember someone who has died? How do we know when to prepare our homes for Passover? On which Shabbat will your Bar Mitzvah be celebrated?

We have our own special way of counting time. Just like any calendar, the Jewish calendar divides the year into days, weeks and months—but our calendar is different in some very important ways.

How do we measure Jewish time?

It is easy to count days. The sun rises in the morning and sets at night. The sun tells us when a day begins and when a day ends. Jews count one day as sundown to sundown. We have counted that way since Bible times. That is why our holidays always begin in the evening.

Time To Light The Lights

We light the Shabbat candles on Friday evening before sunset. But the sun goes down at different times in different places. Jewish calendars have charts to tell us what time to light the candles. Use this chart to fill in the time on the clocks in the pictures.

FRIDAY, JANUARY 19

PLACE	CANDLELIGHTING TIME
BOSTON, MASSACHUSETTS	4:36
CHICAGO, ILLINOIS	4:44
DENVER, COLORADO	4:59
HOUSTON, TEXAS	5:43
LOS ANGELES, CALIFORNIA	5:06

A week is seven days. Jewish days do not have names, except for one very important day. Sunday is called the "First Day" of the week. Monday is the "Second Day," and so on. Only the seventh day, Shabbat, is called by name. We count our weeks from the First Day to Shabbat—seven days.

HOUSTON, TEXAS

BOSTON, MASSACHUSETTS

DENVER, COLORADO

LOS ANGELES, CALIFORNIA

We measure our months by the moon. Every 29½ days a new moon appears in the night sky. It is a very thin crescent moon. As the days go by, the moon grows rounder and rounder until it is shaped like a ball, a full moon. Then it shrinks slowly back into a crescent until it disappears entirely. The changing moons are easy to see and easy to count. We call each complete change, from new moon to new moon, a month. Jewish months are 29 or 30 days long.

בָּרוּךְ אַתָּה יְיָ אֱלֹהֵינוּ מֶלֶךְ הָעוֹלָם
אֲשֶׁר קִדְּשָׁנוּ בְּמִצְוֹתָיו וְצִוָּנוּ
לְהַדְלִיק נֵר שֶׁל שַׁבָּת.

Blessed are You, Lord our God, Ruler of the universe, who has made us holy by giving us His commandments, and has commanded us to kindle the Sabbath lights.

What is Rosh Hodesh?

When the new moon appears it is called **Rosh Hodesh,** which means the beginning of the month. Rosh Hodesh is a kind of holiday. On the Shabbat that comes right before the appearance of the new moon, we say a special prayer. On Rosh Hodesh, the Torah is read in the synagogue. We recite Hallel, a collection of psalms which praise God and ask for God's blessing. We hope that the new month will bring good things to us and to all people.

There are 49 days between Passover and Shavuot. We begin counting on the second day of Passover. This is called counting the **omer.** To count these seven weeks, we have a special omer calendar. This glass and silver one was made in France more than 200 years ago.

The seasons of the year go according to the sun. It is cold in the winter when the sun is low in the sky, and hot in the summer when the sun is high. If we counted only moon months, our holidays would soon come during the wrong seasons. For example, the Bible commands us to celebrate Passover in the spring, when barley ripens in the land of Israel. If we counted time only by the moon, Passover would soon move to wintertime. So we have a Jewish leap year. In a Jewish leap year, we don't just add one day, like February 29th. Every two or three years, we add a whole month!

Every Rosh Hashanah, the Jewish New Year, we increase the number of the year by one. Our everyday calendar tells us that the year is nineteen hundred and "something." Our Jewish calendar tells us that the year is five thousand seven hundred and "something." We count the years all the way back to the beginning of the Bible.

153

The Jewish year begins in the fall as the leaves change color and fall from the trees.

Learn The Months

Look at the box above. Can you memorize the names of the 12 Hebrew months?

This sentence might help you remember the correct order:

THE HAPPY KANGAROO TOOK SALT AND NUTS INTO SEVEN TREES AROUND EGYPT.

Can you write your own "memory" sentence?

		K _____
	H _____	
T _____	S _____	
T _____	N _____	T _____
A _____	S _____	
I _____	E _____	.
A _____		

We begin the new year with the month of Tishre. Rosh Hashanah is the first day in the month of Tishre, New Year's Day. Yom Kippur, Sukkot and Simḥat Torah are all celebrated during Tishre, a busy holiday month. Ḥanukkah begins on the 25th day of the month of Kislev. We light candles for eight nights. When the holiday ends, we are in the next month. Do you know its name?

Tu bi-Shevat, the New Year for Trees, takes its name from the date of its celebration. Tu bi-Shevat means "the 15th day of the month of Shevat." The 14th day of the month of Adar is the merriest day of the Jewish year. Do you know the name of this holiday? Passover begins on the 15th day of the month of Nisan. Many young people are surprised to learn that Nisan is actually the first month of the year! We count 49 days between the second day of Passover and the holiday of Shavuot. In which month do we celebrate Shavuot?

On the 15th day of the month of Shevat—**Tu bi-Shevat**—we celebrate the New Year of the Trees. It is a day for planting trees in Israel. When we plant a tree we make the world a better place. We share in the great work of God's creation.

Monthly Planner

Write the name of each holiday in the month it is celebrated. Remember: Some holidays come in the same month, while other months do not have a holiday.

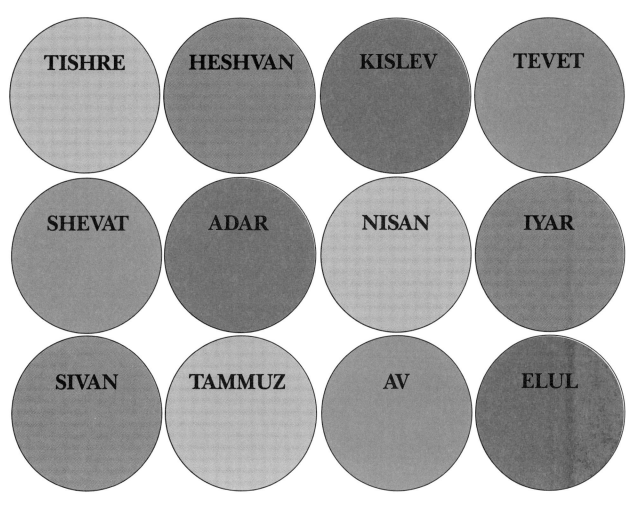

PASSOVER   ROSH HASHANAH   ḤANUKKAH   SIMḤAT TORAH   PURIM
SUKKOT   TU BI-SHEVAT   SHAVUOT   TISHA B'AV   YOM KIPPUR

CHALLENGE: Find out when these holidays are celebrated, and write them on the calendar too.

YOM HASHOAH (A day set aside to remember the Holocaust)
YOM HA'ATZMAUT (Israel's Independence Day)
LAG B'OMER (A special day for school children)
YOUR HEBREW BIRTHDAY

The Jewish calendar binds our people together. Even though we may live in different places, far away from one another, we all celebrate together. All over the world, Jews go to synagogues to celebrate Rosh Hashanah on the very same day. Jews in Israel and in Canada sit down at the Passover seder table on the very same night. Jews in South Africa and in Brazil read the Ten Commandments on Shavuot. Jewish children in England and in Australia hear the Megillah on Purim. When you light the candles on Ḥanukkah, you can be sure that other Jewish children around the world are kindling the Ḥanukkah lights in their homes too, just like you!

Photographic Credits

The editor and publisher gratefully acknowledge the cooperation of the following sources of photographs for this book:

Bill Aron Photography, 9, 63, 66, 105, 109, 111, 112, 114, 121, 125, 131, 141, 154; Michah Bar-Am/Magnum, 91; Devra and Joel Bender, 134; Central Queens YM-YWHA, 51 (bottom left and bottom right), 54; Benjamin Joseph Cutter, 48; Rabbi William Cutter, 65 (bottom right); Daughters of Israel Geriatric Center, 59; Djindjihashvili/ Magnum, 144; Gary Faber/Image Bank, 158; Alan Felix/FourByFive, 95; Cantor Mordecai M. Goldstein, 19; Hebrew Union College-Jewish Institute of Religion, 13, 15, 16, 22 (right); Hebrew Union College-Skirball Museum, 99, 153; Tana Hoban, 80; Jewish National Fund, 146, 156; Esther Kravitz, 51, 53; Shelley Kusnetz, 27; Renee Levine, 61 (bottom); George Mott, 43; Tsuneo Nakamura/FourByFive, 142; Richard Nowitz/Black Star, 36; Ilene Perlman, 22 (left), 24, 25, 28, 30, 37, 61 (top); Dan Porges/Peter Arnold Inc., 103; Zev Radovan/Biblical Archaeology Society, 84; Seymour Rossel, 44; Richard Rowan/Photo Researchers, 127; Rich Russo Photography, 45, 116–117, 128, 142, 145; Clare Sieffert, 47, 78, 79, 85, 89, 97, 100, 101, 102, 124, 136, 152; Sepp Sietz/Woodfin Camp & Associates, 10; Leni Sonnenfeld, 62; Sandi and Thomas Strauss, 12; United Federation of MetroWest, 34, 51, 52, 56, 65, 132; Steven Vidler/FourByFive, 32; Y Country Day Camp Flanders New Jersey, 67, 70, 71, 74, 75.

nas